ENGLAND'S NORTHWEST

AND THE BATTLE FOR SUSTAINABLE DEVELOPMENT
Walter Menzies

© Walter Menzies 2014

Walter Menzies has asserted his rights under the Copyright, Designs and Patent Act 1988 to be identified as the author of this work.

Published by Hector Press
an imprint of Walter Menzies Ltd
www.waltermenzies.co.uk

ISBN 978-1494945046

Cover design by Textbook Studio www.textbookstudio.co.uk
Typesetting by Elaine Sharples www.typesetter.org.uk

"And I will tell you now, if you want to keep your guns, your property, your children and your God…if you love liberty…then sustainable development is your enemy!"
Tom DeWeese

ACKNOWLEDGEMENTS

The contents of this book appeared over a long period, in various forms, in various media. They were published or otherwise disseminated by the following:
A Magazine, Architectural Design, ARUP, *Atlantic Gateway, Building Design, Bollington Live, eg magazine, Green Futures, Green Places,* Groundwork, IPPR, *Guardian, Guardian Public, Manchester Transmission,* Mersey Basin Campaign, *Mersey Minis, North West Enquirer, Place North West, Platform Manchester, RIBA Journal,* SURF, *'sustain,* Sustainability Northwest, Sustainable Development Commission, *Town Planning Review,* University of Liverpool.

Thanks to all of the organisations I have in some way been associated with in the search for sustainability including :
Atlantic Gateway Partnership, Canal and River Trust, CIWEM, Common Purpose, Comtechsa, Creative Concern, Groundwork, Healthy Waterways Trust, Keep Britain Tidy, Land Trust, Manchester and Pennine Waterway Partnership, MIH (Riverside), Mersey Basin Campaign, Morecambe Bay Partnership, Northwest Development Agency, Peel Group, Places Matter!, Renew, SURF, Stockley, Sustainability Northwest, Sustainable Development Commission, University of Liverpool, Waterwise.

And most important of all, tear-jerking thanks to all of the individuals – far too many to mention – who have made it all such fun – you know who you are!

CONTENTS

	INTRODUCTION: PLACE MATTERS	1
1	**SPACESHIP EARTH: OPERATING MANUAL FOUND**	**5**
	An audience with Jonathon Porritt (2003)	7
	One of us or one of them? (2005)	10
	Dark skies: economic development superseded	14
	Time to wake up to the S word (2007)	18
2	**GRIM DOWN SOUTH?**	**21**
	It's grim down south (2006)	23
	The Northwest is booming: grim down south (2006)	26
	Grimmer down south (2007)	28
3	**ENGLAND'S NORTHWEST: BIRTH AND DEATH**	**31**
	An idea whose time has come (2001)	33
	Margins to mainstream (2005)	44
	Manchester is the new Venice (2006)	49
	England's Northwest: over but not out (2011)	52
4	**PARTNERSHIP – THE AEROSOL WORD**	**55**
	Spray it again (2007)	57
	Linking town with country (2012)	60
	Sticking up for partnership (2007)	66
	Partnership: no one said it would be easy (2010)	67
5	**WHITEWASHING THE YARD: REGENERATION**	**77**
	Everything you wanted to know about regeneration (2007)	79
	Environmental improvement (1978):	82
	Beyond bollards (1977)	92
	Producing the goods (2006)	93
	The punctuation marks of history (2008)	96
	Winning – in 2008 (2007)	98

6	**BANNED WORDS AND BULLSHIT BINGO**	101
	Archispeak (1974)	102
	Banned! (2008)	105
	What's in a name? (2008)	108
7	**ART WILL SAVE THE WORLD**	111
	But is it art? (2007)	112
	Eyes wide shut: a golden age of public art (2006)	115
	How do you want your city?	118
8	**ORIGINAL MODERN...AND RAINING: MANCHESTER**	121
	A walk on the wild side (2008)	123
	Manchester: capital of the north's waterways? (2013)	124
	And on the sixth day (2008)	126
	Upward spiral or long descent? (2012)	129
	Hear today (2007)	144
9	**THE POOL OF LIFE: LIVERPOOL**	147
	A new kind of neutron bomb (1978)	149
	Vanishing townscape (1978)	154
	Shot dead (2007)	156
	Hard times: it took a riot (2012)	157
	City region 2030 (2011)	162
	Tomorrow's city: can the private sector deliver? (2012)	170
10	**RIVER THAT CHANGED THE WORLD: MERSEY**	173
	What's the Mersey done for us? (2007)	174
	Message to the planet (2009)	177
	2010: the end of a twenty-five year campaign (2010)	183
11	**LIVERPOOL MEETS MANCHESTER: ATLANTIC GATEWAY**	185
	Top down meets bottom up (2013)	187
	Transformational change (2013)	192
	Atlantic Gateway 2030 (2012)	200
	REFERENCES	211

INTRODUCTION: PLACE MATTERS

"A word to the wise is infuriating"
Dr. Hunter S. Thompson

People matter. Time matters. Space matters…and place matters. This collection is themed around the concept of place and its sustainable development. The place is England's Northwest. Everything connects: we now know that a beautiful butterfly flapping its wings in a rainforest in Borneo is one element in a chain reaction through to a hot pie being eaten in Wigan.

    White Nancy – what a prospect from this icon! New York has its Statue of Liberty, Paris its Eiffel Tower and Edinburgh its Castle. We, in Bollington, where I have lived longer than anywhere else, look up to White Nancy, poised like a rocket revving for take-off on Kerridge Ridge. Above us only sky, crisscrossed with vapour trails from Manchester Airport, jetting the binge flyers across the planet. To the East – the wild green hills of the Peak Park. To the West – in the distance and on a clear day – Fiddlers Ferry Power Station blasts its steam into the atmosphere. To the North – the bling of Beetham Tower pokes above Manchester's city centre haze. To the south – and mercifully out of sight – the city state of London and the South East. And below – the stately Clarence Mill and the Macclesfield Canal remind us that this small corner of England's Northwest was part of the first region in the world to industrialise on an epic scale.

    England's Northwest – the region – is now obliterated from the political map but the place remains in all its complexity and contradictions. Northwest here means Cumbria, Lancashire, Merseyside and Greater Manchester.

Perhaps this collection will be of interest to a few within the dwindling cabal of enthusiasts for the idea of sustainable development in TAFKAR (the Areas Formerly Known as Regions – a Whitehall in-joke). One unforgettable moment in considering audiences was back in 2007 when we at The Mersey Basin Campaign were briefing the distinguished authors for the book *"Mersey The River That Changed The World"* – our contribution to Liverpool's year as European Capital of Culture. We felt that "the creatives" were happier fuelled by booze and so we sat around the boardroom table at Fourways House Eco-Hub drinking cheap wine. *"What's our tone of voice?"* was reasonably asked. The fabulous Anthony Wilson – Mr. Manchester – responded: *"When Sid Vicious was asked if his music was for the man in the street he said to me 'I've met the man in the street and he's a c***' – write for who you want".*

So, there you have it, dear reader. But some explanation may help. In *"Why I Write"*, his brilliant 1947 essay, George Orwell suggests that there are four great motives for writing and *"...in any one writer the proportions will vary from time to time according to the atmosphere in which he is living"*. That certainly applies in my case. These pieces span decades and have been written wearing many different hats.

The motives:
- *"Sheer egoism"*: yes, writing and another of my pleasures – ranting at conferences – are ego trips
- *"Aesthetic enthusiasm"*: yes, there is a buzz in working through from idea to structure to fine-tuning a text
- *"Historical impulse"*: Orwell speaks of the desire to see things as they are – yes, I've been conscious of trying to capture a moment, idea or event

- *"Political purpose"*: here he hits the nail firmly on the head *"...desire to push the world in a certain direction, to alter people's ideas of the kind of society they should strive after"* – yes, I believe more strongly than ever that our society continues to lurch towards Armageddon and that there is an answer – sustainable development, the only credible way of organising our society, economy and environment.

None of the pieces here have been rewritten or edited. I resisted the temptation. Uncut and of their time, they are very different in style, shaped by the medium and the message. Gonzo in that I was part of the story, less than gonzo in that I was always restrained by working within the system in a series of leadership jobs.

The reason that this collection is subtitled *"and the battle for sustainable development"* is that we are in a battle against business as usual, inertia, stupidity and denial. During my time as an advocate and activist here in the Northwest, we have regressed from sustainable development as an idea whose time has come back to the margins. Could I/we have achieved more? Of course – the story is littered with wrong turnings and mistakes. And, ironically, these have been perpetrated by my generation here in one of the richest nations on Earth. A generation uniquely blessed in the entire history of civilisation – with education, affluence, freedom from being wiped out in war and unprecedented professional and personal opportunity. So much to be thankful for and so many people to thank. I hope that this collection avoids Churchill's scathing:

"Take that pudding away – it has no theme".

Walter Menzies, Bollington 2014

1 SPACESHIP EARTH: OPERATING MANUAL FOUND

We are all the ashes of long dead stars. Geological time underlines our total insignificance. As recently as 1963, R. Buckminster Fuller in his *"Operating Manual for Spaceship Earth"* explained that one problem with our marvellous blue planet was its lost operating manual. Not any more. My generation was the first to see images of Earth from space and the first to begin to understand our devastating impact on the Earth's climate. The manual has been found. Or at least enough of it to be sure that we are heading for Armageddon unless the controls are reset.

We have a choice. Sustainable development is the only credible way of organising our environment, economy and society. In the UK, the Sustainable Development Commission worked for a decade as a thought leader and "critical friend" of government. I was fortunate to be appointed as a Commissioner in 2000, from the beginning.

PROVOCATION (2000) was my attempt at a first, short, snappy position statement to help get the ball rolling – all of the Commissioners were asked to nail their colours to the mast. Sadly, it's lost.

The Commission's first Chair – a prime-ministerial appointment by Tony Blair – was Jonathon Porritt. He was – and is – an inspiring leader and speaker, guaranteed to energise the most cynical and defeated audience. By 2003, I had left Sustainability Northwest – the region's advocacy partnership – but was asked to introduce Jonathon P. at a rally for the region's sustainability troops at the glittering new Lowry in Salford: heady days, New Labour fresh, regionalisation blossoming and the concept of sustainable development shifting from the margins into the mainstream. AN AUDIENCE WITH JONATHON PORRITT is a transcript of my rambling attempt to set the scene.

A fundamental difference, I believed, between a sustainable development worldview and a hackneyed "Green" worldview was that economics and business needed to become part of the solution. Porritt's brilliant book *"Capitalism as if the World Matters"* was ahead of its time in exploring this territory. My review, ONE OF US (for *'sustain* magazine in 2005) considered sustainable development activism and claimed that this was the book of the new century.

I knew that the "Greens" tended to shoot themselves in the foot. Their default mode was self-righteous, narrow, dull and boring. I was even more aggravated by the expanding public sector "economic development" industry – a toxic gang of chancers. I enjoyed every opportunity to take a pop at them from public platforms, deriding their roundabouts / crinkly sheds / inward investment school of thought. DARK SKIES – notes for some talk or another – I can't remember where or when and it doesn't matter – was a typical outburst from me.

Businesses enjoy competing. We exploited this for years through The Northwest Business Environment Awards – an initiative that I enjoyed leading. Year after year we found companies – large and small – that were genuinely raising the bar. TIME TO WAKE UP TO THE S WORD was a plug – and a provocation – written for the Northwest RIBA's fine *A magazine* in 2007.

AN AUDIENCE WITH JONATHON PORRITT (2003)

Well, thanks very much Steven, and to you and the NWDA for supporting this glittering occasion with a fantastic cast of characters, with ladies and gentlemen and lords as well: Terry, you are particularly welcome tonight. Maybe other lords, at least one distinguished lord. This is part of Mersey Basin Week: 170 events going on across the region as we speak involving many different people in many places. Mrs Thatcher said the community's dead – no it's not. A vast amount of activity still goes on.

A brief ad on the region and then I'll welcome Jonathon. The ad is for the Northwest Business Environment Awards, the region's premier award scheme supported by the NWDA, the CBI and our friends in Envirolink, ENWORKS and the Environment Agency. Take a leaflet and win an award. Well worth doing. Massive and exotic ceremony next April that nobody can possibly miss.

Well, welcome Jonathon to England's Northwest, a region that it has been said on various occasions has more visions than St Theresa, more pilots than the RAF, and increasingly more partnerships than the entire chartered accountancy profession. Important though you are, you're not the first VIP to come here. Queen Victoria opened the Manchester Docks here in 1894 and this is where we are now. The Manchester Docks became the third biggest port in the country, in the UK, and the story of what we now know as the Quays has been quite extraordinary. A catastrophic decline of the docks in the 70s: more than 3,000 jobs were lost. In 1982 the docks closed altogether. Leaving serious dereliction, contamination and the water in the Ship Canal heavily polluted. At that time, Salford City Council could not give away the land to developers, things had reached such a low ebb.

I think where we are now demonstrates energy, ambition and vision – we've achieved really quite phenomenal things and a huge transformation in the last 20 years here at the Quays. By the mid 90s, more than £35 millions of public money had been spent on land reclamation here. The first £250 million of private investment had been secured and in 1999 the Metrolink linked the Quays to the city centre – a sustainable transport link. In 2000 the Lowry opened and against all the whingeing of the moaning minnies became a huge success from the very beginning. With more than one million people coming through the doors in the first twelve months and continuing success it is a fantastic icon for the Northwest region. In 2002, a highlight of the Commonwealth Games was the triathlon here. Swimmers out there in the water, 40,000 people came, and of course the same year the Imperial War Museum was opened.

As we speak, an innovative oxygenation plant is keeping the waters clean and The Campaign will soon be announcing really quite spectacular results in terms of improvements to the biodiversity in the waters out there. So this really is an icon of Northwest innovation, ambition, regeneration. Hugely improved water quality, new jobs, and marvellous facilities for local people and visitors.

But there is no room at all for complacency. The Northwest, as Steven said, still has huge challenges, economic, social and environmental. Within a mile of here there is housing still being abandoned. Something like 400,000 local authority homes are suffering from low demand in the Northwest region. Merseyside's GDP is still such that it is a European Objective 1 area, although you'll point out I'm sure, Jonathon, that GDP is not the only intelligent measure, it is still a factor to consider. The Northwest still has derelict land equivalent to nearly eight cities the size of Preston, a huge amount of derelict land to deal with to turn this region round. One million adults have literacy difficulties, and here's a real cracker – the NDA will be spending a staggering sum of £40 billion in this region on nuclear decommissioning. So big challenges, but there are fantastic examples of creativity, of innovation, of ambition amongst all of those working for a sustainable region. We haven't quite got there yet, we haven't quite overpowered the forces of darkness, but many things are moving in the correct direction.

Now Jonathon Porritt, you don't need much introduction from me. In fact there are 7,360 Jonathon Porritt references on Google on the Web if you want to find out more about what Jonathon has been up to over recent years, and he's been up to a very great deal. He is of course Chair of the Government's Sustainable Development Commission, Advisor to the PM, appointed by the PM and happy to point the government in the correct direction. He is still Co-director of Forum for the Future and an advisor to major companies. The Forum's *Green Futures* is a magazine you should all read. Many other things as well: broadcasting, writing and most important of all I think inspiring people to see that sustainable development is the only sensible way of organising ourselves. So without further waffle from me, a very warm welcome to Jonathon Porritt.

ONE OF US OR ONE OF THEM? (2005)

One of Mrs Thatcher's more helpful contributions to the delivery of sustainable development was her idea of "one of us" or "one of them". *"Is he one of us?"* the Prime Minister would fiercely enquire about candidates for jobs. Only those who passed the test were admitted to the top table. Party membership was not nearly enough. The old guard were out.

The radical transformation to a low-carbon society is more challenging than the Thatcherite revolution. And not everybody is a sustainable development activist – one of us. There are many easy demons: *"And I will tell you now, if you want to keep your guns, your property, your children and your God...if you love liberty...then sustainable development is your enemy!"* rants Tom DeWeese of the American Policy Centre. Nearer to home, my favourite list of bads includes – toddler crushing SUVs; Jeremy Clarkson; CPRE; David Bellamy; the pixieshit jerry built by volume house builders incapable even of complying with our pitifully timid building regulations; public sector self-righteousness and inertia; the treatment of all business people as suspected criminals; the CBI whingeing about red tape as a problem rather than an opportunity...the list is, of course, endless.

It is very easy to be confused. George Bush's startling State of the Union speech included the pale green confession that *"Americans are addicted to oil"*. The Chinese are opening a coal-fired power station every week. And yet Arup has been commissioned to build the world's first sustainable city at Dongtan, Shanghai. Three-quarters of the size of Manhattan, the aim is carbon neutrality and clean energy from organic waste. James Lovelock, the originator of the Gaia theory of Earth as a living organism – once a hero to many Greens – has become a passionate advocate of nuclear energy. This is the only way to save humanity from climate change, he now claims. New Labour, the Conservatives and the Liberal Democrats jostle for moral supremacy over the environment. And the UK has been ranked fifth best in the world at tackling domestic and global environmental problems, according to the first performance league tables launched in January at the World Economic Forum in Davos.

Is it any wonder that Fiona Harvey – in an otherwise intelligent review in the Financial Times of Jonathon Porritt's *"Capitalism as if the World Matters"* – believes that *"sustainability is a sometimes overused buzzword amongst environmentalists and Green politicians"*?

How do we make sense of these complexities and contradictions? Nobody is better placed to power through the fog than Jonathon Porritt. He has been an influential Green. He has moved on to work closely with business leaders and, as chair of the Sustainable Development Commission, has devoted much of his last five years as the "critical friend" of government.

The big question he sets out to answer is: *"How do we retain capitalism's dynamism, creativity, innovation and hunger for change and progress that has made it one of the most powerful forces in the history of the world and yet stay within biophysical limits?"*

He reminds us that the world now produces – in less than two weeks – the equivalent of the entire physical output of the year 1900. Rather than trickling down, many of the benefits of the global economy *"continue to gush upwards"*. More than 90 per cent of all the materials used to manufacture consumer products end up as waste. Millions of Christian fundamentalists in the US believe that environmental destruction is to be welcomed as a sign of the coming Apocalypse. Here in the UK, 12 per cent of people still live in poverty. Endless surveys show that most people are broadly contented with our greed-driven consumer society even if it doesn't make them happier. Happy people live seven years longer than unhappy people.

He pulls no punches. Business: many directors are in thrall to investors who couldn't give a toss about the companies, let alone their employees, their communities or the environment. Some are diverted by the *"empty seductive illusion"* that is corporate social responsibility. This should be a set text for the ever-expanding CSR industry.

Government: the progressive left is incapable of thinking beyond the myth that permanent economic growth is the answer to everything. Symptoms, not systems, remain the order of the day.

Environmentalists: have completely lost the plot – *"any mention of the bigger picture...sends them running off to their birdboxes and gently simmering organic lentils"*. A glorious image.

The first part of this book vividly outlines the environmental – and human – crisis that we face. Then he tackles capitalism – his Five Capitals Framework is about interconnecting natural, human, social, manufactured and financial capital. He outlines the business case for sustainable development: *"The transition presents new opportunities for entrepreneurs, new sources of economic prosperity and jobs, a higher quality of life for people, safer, more secure communities, a better work-life balance and so on..."*

Confronting denial – the final section of the book – analyses the reasons for inaction, explores new ways of measuring progress beyond the bottom line, and presents positive visions and principles.

This book untangles the widespread and damaging misconception that sustainable development is some sort of reactionary, dreary, Green project. Unlike conventional environmentalism, sustainable development is as much about the wellbeing of the human species as about the wellbeing of the natural world. It is also about progress, enterprise, innovation and creativity rather than muesli, cardigans, slogans and Stalinism. Porritt's take on capitalism as if the world matters is compelling: *"an evolved, intelligent and elegant form of capitalism that puts the earth at its very centre (as our one and only world) and ensures that all people are its beneficiaries in recognition of our unavoidable interdependence".*

He neglects the critical subject of leadership for sustainable development – a good subject for the next book, maybe. And I would have enjoyed an exploration of the English rural economy: eye-watering subsidies and Volvo driving, tweed-and-Laura-Ashley clad National Trust members standing in the way of progress with their misconception that the English landscape is "natural".

And he doesn't explore the corridors of Whitehall – not, I think, because the story is too bleak and shocking for all but the most hardened readers – but because he still has important work to do there.

Sustainable development is the only credible theory that can be used to confront the challenge. And there is nothing so practical as a good theory. For those of us attempting sustainability literacy, *"Capitalism as if the World Matters"* is the book of the century.

Sustainable development activists will not settle for acceptance of a dark, Mad Max vision of the future. Reading *'sustain* magazine, with its emphasis on solutions, is a more enjoyable way of becoming "one of us". People are more important than newts. iPods are more beautiful than potpourri. Wind farms are more inspiring than ramblers. Any organisation or logo using the word or colour "green" needs to wake up and join us in the twenty-first century. Less is more. Time is short.

Capitalism – As if the World Matters
by Jonathon Porritt
Earthscan, 2005

DARK SKIES: ECONOMIC DEVELOPMENT SUPERSEDED

Why has the sky gone dark and what is that flapping sound?
- The sky is dark with black swans coming home to roost, and if one of them poos on you, tough!
- Unleashed by our friends in economic development
- It's Apocalypse time – the boys in striped shirts and red braces have presided over what has been described as:

"The greatest episode of value destruction the world has ever known outside two world wars"

The human fallout has been devastating:
- People have lost jobs
- People have lost homes
- Others are trapped in negative equity
- Or find their pensions worthless

But that's international corporates and bankers and politicians and regulators who've failed – you say. Let's come closer to home then, to England's Northwest and inspect the wreckage here…

What's that over there?
- It's a roundabout leading to an inward investment site, the pinnacle of achievement for local authority economic development
- Look – feral youths and McDonalds cartons blowing about and over there the crinkly shed – yes, it's a Pets-R-Us – a prison for harmless puppies
- Welcome to the world of local economic development – a fantasy parallel universe dreamed up by people in local authorities and assorted quangos

These are the people:
- who want to build a bridge across the bay to Barrow – they haven't managed to work out that this would enable the population to escape even faster
- who want to build roads – did you know that if only 10% of the national roads budget was set aside it could finance:
  - 40 new parks
  - Half a million street trees
  - 1.5 million sq.ft of green roofs
  - 1000 miles of safe greenway for bikes and pedestrians?
- who believe that the height of ambition for Manchester is to achieve the same level of GVA as London, not realising that:
  - A GCSE-level economics student would know how absurd this is
  - It's grim down south and we don't WANT to be like London
- who think that shopping is the new shipping and that "retail led" regeneration is the answer: spend, spend, spend and consume more and more stuff to save ourselves
- who inhabit a deranged netherworld of hallucinations, meeting after meeting about:
  - Economic assessment duties
  - Outcomes
  - Multi-area agreements
  - Inward investment
  - MIPIM (Massive Pissups in the Mediterranean)
  - Local economic strategies
- whose professional institute claims as hot question of the moment – and I am not making this up:

"How do you resolve ambiguities within and between national policy objectives investment and resource allocation decisions and

delivery practice at local level where managing the holistic approach in implementation has proved difficult?"

Well, I have news for them — the arcane technical term I would use is BOLLOX

Look at the wonderful achievements:
- Inequalities – greater in all OECD countries, including Britain, compared to 20 years ago – a period of unparallelled economic growth
- Global economy has doubled in the last 20 years but the increase in resources consumption has degraded an estimated 60% of the world's ecosystem and accelerated the pace of catastrophic climate change
- Those who suffer most are the poorest – Kofi Annan recently claimed that today's world ALREADY has as many environmental migrants as refugees

The economic development people are in denial about two simple facts, obvious I am sure to everybody in this room:
- The economy is the wholly-owned subsidiary of the environment
- There is no credible model of a socially just, ecologically sustainable scenario of endless growing income and consumption for a world heading towards 9 million people

Economic development has failed catastrophically – the market has been undone by growth itself

And the answer?
Now is the time for the idea whose time has come – sustainable development – an organising principle for society that has a triple bottom line: environmental, social and economic

So, I say to our friends in economic development:
There are many ways in which you could retrain so as to help make the world a better place, still within the comfortable world of local authorities:
- As park-keepers perhaps, making our parks safer and greener
- As teachers – of proper subjects like science or languages
- As binmen – improving refuse collection

Economic development – superseded!

TIME TO WAKE UP TO THE S WORD (2007)

Fifteen ear-popping seconds in the lift to the Manchester Hilton Cloud 23 Bar – cocktails, sparkle, bling and the glittering night cityscape below. Sirens wail. Lights blaze from emptying offices. Endless streams of dinky cars head off to the suburbs and beyond. From this thrilling vantage point, no need to slip on the magic night shades to get the picture: a huge pall of CO_2 blasting into the stratosphere. The soundtrack? It has to be Kermit the Frog with the unforgettable *"It ain't easy bein' green"*.

Lighting and heating buildings generates 50 per cent of Britain's carbon dioxide emissions. Producing building materials accounts for a further 10 per cent. The construction industry generates one third of all waste in Britain. Twenty per cent of new building materials in the average building site are dumped. Some 13 million tonnes of new materials are thrown away each year – the equivalent of 88 Giza pyramids. Office blocks, dating back to the 1960s, are being bulldozed to create floorplates for financial sector suits. Volume housebuilders continue to trash the environment with low density pixieshit designed for car-dependent lives.

Then there is the existing building stock – 75 per cent of the UK's existing homes are expected to be here in 2050. Homes are responsible for 27 per cent of our CO_2 emissions. Most of them are energy inefficient, nine million with no cavity wall insulation. Fuel poverty is a growing problem. Disincentives to retrofit action include VAT on refurbishment.

Sustainable communities? Pass the sick bag and I'll dump it out of the window of this speeding SUV. The development and construction sector is not at the forefront of the low carbon economy. As for design: Victor Papanek pointed out that an obsession with making things pretty is a crime against humanity.

There are signs of progress though. The new UK Green Buildings Council, launched at Ecobuild, has heavyweight members. Peter Rogers of Stanhope, its chair, says: *"There needs to be three zeros — zero carbon, zero water and zero waste... changes will have to be driven by the industry as government legislation would take too long."* Its mission is to *"dramatically improve the sustainability of the built environment by radically transforming the way it is planned, designed, constructed, maintained and operated."*

The guide to sustainable buildings in the Northwest is still so flimsy as to be unpublishable. But there are a small but growing number of heroes at every stage of the development process – clients, architects and other professionals. Be inspired by the winners in the built environment category of this year's *North West Business Environment Awards*, featured elsewhere in this magazine.

Buckminster Fuller pointed out, a generation ago, that no instruction book came with spaceship Earth. Now we have worked out enough of the instructions to know that we can't carry on like this. Climate change is dragging the S Word – sustainability – from the margins to the mainstream. New soundtrack?

2 GRIM DOWN SOUTH?

England's Northwest was, and remains, different from London and its suburbs – most of southern England and Birmingham. Now London is morphing into an overheated, offshore city state. Edinburgh is the capital of Scotland. Manchester will become the natural capital of England. In the decade of regionalism – roughly the first ten years of this century – there was endless talk of "North/South divide", "bridging the productivity gap" and more recently "rebalancing the economy". I have tried to play my part by endlessly repeating that we are not the South. Basingstoke is not the greatest achievement of world civilisation. There is another, a better way.

Perhaps the most inspired strike of our gone, but not forgotten, Northwest Development Agency was its inspired *"Grim Down South"* campaign. To promote our region to the captains of industry attending the 2004 CBI Conference in Manchester, *"It's Grim Down South"* tags were hung on the doors of the city's four and five-star hotel rooms. Huge success – Sir Humphrey empurpled with rage and terrific media coverage. I've been enthusiastically promoting the *"Grim Down South"* brand ever since.

I wrote IT'S GRIM DOWN SOUTH for the first ever edition of *North West Enquirer* in 2006, a courageous attempt at an intelligent regional broadsheet newspaper. I was keen on the idea of *Enquirer* as a new focus for the Northwest Regional Project. Sadly, it had a short life.

Simon Jenkins is occasionally entertaining as a *Guardian* columnist. His opinions about regeneration in our region were exceptionally inaccurate and flaky in one misguided piece in 2006. I wrote THE NORTHWEST IS BOOMING: GRIM DOWN SOUTH as a riposte. At least they published it.

City rankings, indices and comparisons are alway enjoyable, however absurd. It's the nerdy excitement of lists. GRIMMER DOWN SOUTH was an online column for *Place North West* triggered by the Royal Bank of Scotland's 2007 *"Affordable Affluence Index"*. We were not to know of the Bank's looming contribution to the destruction of affluence on a devastating, world-class scale.

IT'S GRIM DOWN SOUTH (2006)

It's grim down south. On Surrey stockbrokers' gravel drives, Chelsea tractors are unloved and dusty after the school run. Sunday mornings stretch interminably for Essex girls and boys, their GTIs unwashed. Retired colonels in Folkestone keep stiff upper lips as their compulsory water meters are installed. They know that their rainfall is less than in much of the Middle East. Supergrasses patrol Kent suburbs and shop their neighbours for illicit nocturnal watering. 13 million people are already banned from using hosepipes and sprinklers. This summer's drought down south may be as serious as anything in living memory.

Water is the new energy, shriek the London media. Unions criticise water companies for selling reservoirs for development. There is talk of towing icebergs from the Arctic. Consumers are warned that they use far more water than their European neighbours and it's time they stopped flushing one third of it down the pan. Engineers dream of building gigantic reservoirs. And the newts on the reserves at Rainham Marshes muse on their future. What will become of them, they wonder, when the Thames Gateway – forty-three miles by twenty miles – engulfs them? It's a flood plain, isn't it? How will the huge demands for drinking water be met?

That's not all. With climate change, sea levels are rising. And Britain is tilting as well. The southeast is sinking. What a vision! Bowler-hatted Sir Humphreys take to the boats, their red tape unfurling chaotically in the abandoned Whitehall corridors. Meanwhile, Wigan Investment Centre rises majestically to its rightful height.

Oop Northwest, our rivers are cleaner than before the Industrial Revolution. The Manchester Ship Canal no longer catches fire. Salmon are returning to the Mersey. Beaches sparkle. Our tap water tastes better and is a hundredth of the rip-off price of bottled water trucked across Europe. Development has turned to face the rivers and canals. Water is a catalyst for regeneration. Think of Salford Quays or New East Manchester or Mersey Waterfront or Preston Docks.

So, should we revel uncharitably at the fate of our friends in the South? Not quite. Water quality: there has been spectacular improvement here since privatisation and the investment must continue. Good for our environment and regeneration, certainly, but it has to be paid for. Water bills must increase. Waterside dereliction: The Northwest has an area of dereliction about the size of Preston. At the present rate it will take centuries to reclaim. The way we live: we don't have as many arid golf courses or three-car households as Surrey. But there is great potential for us to waste less water and the energy that's needed to supply it. Some of the solutions are complicated and need innovation or behaviour change. Others, like water-saving devices in cisterns, are cheap, simple and immediate.

Climate change: the prospect of palm trees in Blackpool and Mediterranean café society in Manchester may be alluring. But our weather is becoming extreme, with more frequent storms and floods. We have a very long coastline and building stronger sea defences is expensive.

Official estimates suggest that floods in the Thames Gateway could damage a staggering £80bn of property. The government recently claimed that it had invested £6bn in transport, health and education projects in the area. There are acute housing and environmental problems in London and the South East. Private housebuilding and the market alone will not solve these. Massive public expenditure is needed to avoid increasingly grim prospects for our friends in the South.

There will be competition for this money. It *is* grim down south but their pain is not necessarily our gain. And do we really want to live like them? Is down south the height of our ambition and imagination? Could the Northern Way be a better way? Could we regenerate our cities in ways that are sustainable? Could we adapt intelligently to climate change? Are we content with Sir Humphrey's unforgettable remark that *"Our responsibility is not to do things, it is to explain why nothing can be done"*?

Skelmersdale is not Dubai. Wilmslow is not Chipping Sodbury. Storm clouds are gathering. As we happily power-jetwash our whippets, we might just like to remind ourselves that this great region of ours, the Northwest, is not an island.

THE NORTHWEST IS BOOMING: GRIM DOWN SOUTH (2006)

The rising north and the sinking south-east isn't just a geological phenomenon.

Simon Jenkins is right – up to a point (*British politics can't survive if it treats provincial cities as overseas colonies*, October 6th). I'm glad that he likes Manchester. But his grasp of regeneration is flaky. How can a city that has grown its city centre population from almost nothing to 15,000 in 15 years be *"the worst advertisement for Labour caucus government"*?

Moss Side is not *"a testament to Jane Jacobs's thesis that architects, not people, make slums"*: much of it is 19th- century terraces. It is not true that *"the city centre pockets of character were saved against the local council"*: the Council designated Castlefield as Britain's first urban heritage park. Rescued from abandonment, it is now a successful mixed-use canalside quarter. The Northern Quarter is an edgy, creative mix of small shops and independent businesses in a brooding Victorian townscape, more vibrant than Covent Garden before it was sanitised by developers.

To claim that *"Salford Quays is a landscape of glass boxes set in tarmac, the same future slums that Manchester built in the 70s"* is absurd. Michael Wilford's Lowry arts centre and Daniel Liebeskind's Imperial War Museum are iconic works of architecture attracting more than three million visits a year – and at a fraction of the price of London's empty Millennium Dome.

The regeneration of the Quays is an inspiring story. Twenty years ago the docks had gone and the land was derelict and had negative value. The Ship Canal was so contaminated that it sometimes caught fire. Public investment in land reclamation and the use of innovative technology in improving the water triggered a transformation. Developers have responded – there are already more than 10,000 new jobs. And this is only the beginning. Work has begun on the development of MediaCity around the arrival of the BBC. Bold leadership by a Labour council (Salford) has been critical.

At the other end of the Ship Canal is Liverpool – a Liberal Democrat council for many years. Jenkins is right about the city's thrilling potential for the old and new *"responding"*. Liverpool's past economic failure saved much of the centre from tacky development. It has more listed buildings than any city outside the capital, as well as the World Heritage asset of its magnificent dock estate. Liverpool's spectacular setting on the Mersey Estuary is much grander than central London on the Thames. The Mersey is now cleaner than at any time since before the Industrial Revolution: salmon have returned.

Sustainable transformation of port cities like Liverpool, or textile cities like Manchester that were devastated by global economic forces, is hugely challenging. Mistakes have been made. There are still far too many jobless people living in poor housing and environments.

But the real story of regeneration needs to be told. The crane count in both Liverpool and Manchester is unprecedented. For most of us it's no longer grim oop north. Geologically, we are rising and the south-east is sinking. Emotionally, we do not aspire to the overheated South-East. In fact, many of us think that it's grim down south.

GRIMMER DOWN SOUTH (2007)

An endless stream of surveys commissioned by anyone from bankers to energy providers tells us to favour one town or city over another, but is it sensible to take any notice of such gauges?

Oh no, not another chip on the Northwest shoulder?
No. Only three of the twenty towns in a recent *"Affordable Affluence Index"* are in the South East and we have two in the top twenty – Chester at number three and Salford at number five. This new index is from the Royal Bank of Scotland, no less.

Where's the evidence?
Banks are not noted for their imagination. They mapped a data model to identify hotspots of affluent lifestyle indicators. These ranged from schools to entertainment facilities to house prices. Salford's strengths in culture and sport and some very affordable areas make it an attractive choice for the affluent. By affluent, RBS mean incomes of £100,000 plus.

But how does this relate to the famous 'crap towns' survey?
Quite well. 20,000 people voted for crap towns. Three were in the South East – Luton, Windsor and Clapham. Happily, no Northwest town made the worst ten.

And the tower crane / hairdresser count?
This really is the way to compare towns and cities. Well, according to one distinguished economist after a few drinks. Count the tower cranes. Dig out the figures on the rate of bankruptcy of hairdressers. There is a direct correlation between the frequency of visiting the hairdresser and prosperity.

Economic performance isn't everything, though?
How very true. Leading gurus like Richard Florida are piling up more and more evidence that economic comparisons of towns and cities are false gods. It's the quality of life, stupid. And well-being and creativity

Creativity?
Yes. Manchester topped the *"Boho Britain Creativity Index"*, ahead of London. This ranked the creative potential of cities. Manchester has an exceptionally rich mix of ethnic diversity, gay friendliness and technological innovation. And new ideas need old buildings. Yes, there are still problems. The City Council's newly-published 70-page *"State of the City Report"* tells the story, warts and all. A compelling headline is that the "age of flight" seems to be over: since 2001, Manchester's population has been increasing at twice the national average.

Are our towns not famed for their creativity?
"When a place gets boring, even the rich people leave" the great urbanist Jane Jacobs pointed out. *"Clone Town Britain"* already describes 42 per cent of UK towns, with a further 26 per cent under threat, according to the New Economics Foundation. Identikit chain stores spread like economic weeds. High streets everywhere become indistinguishable from each other. "Regeneration" can wipe out lively mixes of retailers, pubs and family-owned businesses. Who has not felt deep despair, lost in the wasteland of edge-of-town shedville wondering, *"Where am I? Anywhere? Nowhere? Is parking the new religion?"*

How will climate change affect the relative performance of towns?
In the Middle Ages, the best way of ranking towns was by the number of churches. In the 20th century we discovered

shopping. In the 21st century, it's all about survival. The South East is geologically sinking: the Northwest is rising. Droughts, floods, and extreme weather events are already with us. The Carbon Trust has started mapping the CO_2 outputs of towns and cities. British Gas's ranking of towns by carbon footprint per household named and shamed Crawley. An average of 5,820kg CO_2 a year was emitted for each Crawley household. This is equivalent to the CO_2 generated by driving 25,500km. Scary!

So, is it really grim down south?
Our friends in the South need hope too. It's too easy to knock them. Ludicrous house prices. Hideous commuting. London under water as the Thames Barrier is overwhelmed. That kind of thing. Gloating doesn't get us very far. And we'd all end up paying anyway. The tipping point? Realising that comparing our towns and cities using economic performance alone is yesterday's story. Quality of life will be the new rock n' roll.

3 ENGLAND'S NORTHWEST: BIRTH AND DEATH

One day, the colourful story of the abortive Northwest "Regional Project" will be told. There were heroes and villains as well as 99 per cent of the citizens of this great region of ours who were never aware that they were part of the Regional Project. I was wholeheartedly signed up to it. The coming of New Labour was a glittering new dawn. At the Regional Conference in 1997 we gathered in the sunshine at Low Wood on Lake Windermere as the Red Arrows screamed overhead, their vapour trails painting the sky a new and better colour: red. John Prescott had just told us that Cumbria was in the Northwest (a mixed blessing) and that regions in England had finally arrived.

We knew that the Northwest had a larger population and economy than several EU countries and that we were governed as colonial subjects of Whitehall. We knew that England was one of the most centralised states in the developed world. We knew that Whitehall was completely dysfunctional, its place-blind warring silos dedicated to protecting their ministers' arses. We knew that few of the metrocentric glitterati could find Liverpool or Manchester on a map. Meanwhile, Scotland was thriving on its devolution journey.

My role in the short life of England's Northwest was as an advocate of sustainable regional development – this was not a given. Constant vigilance against the forces of darkness was needed.

AN IDEA WHOSE TIME HAS COME was my contribution to a 2001 IPPR / Green Alliance publication *Sustainable Development and the English Regions*.

MARGINS TO MAINSTREAM was written in 2005 for *eg* a sort of sustainability house magazine for the growing band of local authority and other sustainability people.

MANCHESTER IS THE NEW VENICE was an exploration in 2006 of the shift in thinking from regions towards city regions. Now it is city regions that remain alive and seem to be the future.

ENGLAND'S NORTHWEST: OVER BUT NOT OUT was a short requiem for the death of the regional project and a final act of defiance for the Sustainable Development Commission, axed – alongside hope – by the Cameron/Clegg coalition in 2011.

What happened to the Northwest flag?

AN IDEA WHOSE TIME HAS COME (2001)

Sustainable regional development is an idea whose time has come in Northwest England. This contribution is made from the perspective of the partnership sector and is built on the experience of Sustainability Northwest (SNW). SNW is Europe's first cross-sectoral partnership organisation dedicated to advancing sustainable development at the regional level.

Sustainable development is critical at every level from the global through to the local. Every level is interconnected. There is a regional dimension of many issues – planning, transport, waste, water quality, business clusters, skills and many others.

How is the Northwest progressing towards mainstreaming sustainable development in policies, programmes and delivery? We share the same global, European and national context as the other English regions. But there are some special characteristics. This paper considers the context, the region, the emerging regional machinery and signs of progress. It concludes with some suggestions.

The context

"Sustainable development will need to be seen as a framework linking issues, stressing priorities but not binding itself into a wholesale philosophy. It must itself be de-greened".
Michael Jacobs (1999)

Jacobs's 1999 analysis of the environment as a wicked issue for New Labour and its even greater difficulty with sustainable development has not yet been superseded by changes in national political discourse. The Prime Minister's long-awaited *"Richer and Greener"* speech in October 2000 recognised the need for *"a new approach to the environment... a coalition that works with the grain of consumers, business and science not against them"* (Blair, 2000). It failed to articulate the principles of sustainable development as the integrating principle for environmental, economic, social and democratic progress.

On the credit side, the government has, for instance, produced its annual sustainability report and established the UK's Sustainable Development Commission as a "critical friend".

A second aspect of the regional context is governance, devolution (or the lack of it!) and the centralising tendencies and silo machinery of Whitehall. Peter Kilfoyle MP memorably – and partly unfairly – described the Government Offices for the Regions as *"colonial administrations"*. The North West Constitutional Convention has pointed out that *"Too much of what affects our daily lives is decided for us more than two hundred miles away and implemented by public services which have little or no contact with the public they serve and have no accountability to any democratic body in the region."* (North West Constitutional Convention, 2000). New Labour is deeply divided on the question of devolution.

The most powerful drivers are forces beyond government control – globalisation, industrial innovation and eco-efficiency, scientific breakthroughs and public attitudes to climate change, for instance. However, national government continues to exercise great influence and commands huge resources in the regions: the NHS is the region's largest employer with a budget of £4.4 billion.

The Northwest region

"The landscapes of the Northwest region range between extremes – from the densely populated Mersey Belt to the wilds of

Cumbria...they embrace some of the most beautiful in England to some of the worst, in desperate need of reclamation."
Professor John Handley (SNW, 1997)

The Northwest is a big European region with a GDP of £72.2 billion – greater than that of five European states – and a population of nearly 7 million. As the first world region to industrialise on a massive scale, the Northwest has chalked up some spectacular innovations – from the first passenger railway in the world, to the birth of the modern computer through to world-class standing in rock music and football. MORI found that 600,000 Londoners support Northwest football teams (MORI, 1997). The post-bomb renaissance of Manchester City Centre is an exemplar of urban renaissance. Its population is has risen tenfold over a ten-year period.

But more than 200 years of unsustainable development has left a challenging legacy:

- The economic disparities between the extremes such as West Cumbria and the "Southern Crescent" (a high growth zone across North Cheshire with virtually nil unemployment) are enormous. There are pockets of intense poverty and deprivation including 19 from the DETR's "worst" 50.
- Environmental problems include 25 per cent of England's derelict land and a legacy of poor water quality in the Mersey Basin, although spectacular progress has been made: salmon now leap upstream in the Mersey! Our CO_2 emissions are such that we would have to plant the whole of Cumbria with poplars to absorb 12 per cent of the region's annual greenhouse gas emissions (Northwest Climate Group, 2000)
- The state we are in is most dramatically headlined by health disparities – the seven-year difference in life expectancy between the most affluent and poorest areas remains an affront to an advanced society.

- New challenges now "on agenda" include climate and demographic change: 25 per cent more people aged between 65 and 85 by 2019 (UMIST, 1999).
- Participation in democracy is poor. Average turnout at the last local elections in Liverpool was 22.3 per cent, with some wards managing fewer than 12 per cent. The Liverpool Democracy Commission is, however, addressing this. At the regional level, MORI encouragingly reports that 97 per cent of our citizens know which region they live in, 69 per cent believe that a regional assembly *"would look after the interests of this area better than central government"*. However, a discouraging 58 per cent believe that this would lead to *"more bureaucracy"* and a disturbing figure of only 28 per cent believe that *"Politicians elected to a regional assembly would be more trustworthy than politicians elected to parliament at Westminster"* (The Economist, 1999)

Is our regional machinery up to shaping a sustainable 21st-century future from this point?

The machinery

The Northwest shares – with the other English regions – an incredibly complex and insufficiently connected mosaic of regional institutions, agencies, partnerships and initiatives. Designing from scratch a streamlined public policy / delivery machine to achieve sustainable regional development would not have produced this dog's breakfast. However, countering the tendency towards dysfunction, jockeying for position, crossed wires, the re-invention of wheels, overlap and chaos, there are some significant positives.

While "partnership the aerosol word" – continues to be sprayed on countless initiatives, it is not a novel mode in the Northwest. This was the region that in 1981 invented Groundwork as a pioneer of local regeneration partnerships.

The Mersey Basin Campaign has succeeded in improving water quality. It is an exceptional example of a long-term partnership – set up with a twenty-five year life in recognition of the magnitude of the task. The predecessor body to the North West Regional Assembly was the North West Partnership: this encompassed not only the local authorities but also business and, to a degree, the third sector. So there is long experience of partnership development and working in the region.

Business engagement in sustainable development at the regional level is not new either. For more than ten years the North West Business Leadership Team (NWBLT) which brings together heavy hitters from many of the region's corporates has championed quality of life issues. The NWBLT was instrumental in forming SNW, set up with the specific mission of advancing sustainable regional development.

The powerful health sector is beginning to connect with the sustainability and regeneration agendas. This has enormous potential. For instance, connecting NHS capital investment to regeneration initiatives within a context of sustainable development would be a very big win-win.

In a knowledge economy, the universities have a major role to play in making connections – between themselves and with the regional agenda. While they remain driven by competitive funding and the need to publish in arcane journals, real steps are being taken – for instance by the formation of the North West Universities Association – to connect. Creative collaboration – for instance between academics and SNW on climate change work – has married science with communications and policy development to advance the sustainability cause.

Finally, the establishment of the Northwest Development Agency was widely supported and welcomed across the region, with great expectations of this new force for change.

The strategies

"The Northwest was arguably the first region in the world to pollute the environment on a structured, grand, even imperial scale, in the desire for economic growth. This new millennium will be an age when we can set our sights on reversing that process, based on the principles of sustainable development."

Lord Thomas of Macclesfield, Chair,
Northwest Development Agency (NWDA, 2000)

There have been many analyses of this and other regions' strategies. Our regional suite of strategies includes the Northwest Development Agency-led *Strategy Towards 2020*, draft *Regional Planning Guidance* (NW Regional Assembly, 2000a) and the Regional Sustainability Framework – *Action for Sustainability*. (NW Regional Assembly, 2000b). All emphasise sustainable development as a guiding principle. Many other strategies and action plans are emerging, both thematic (such as the *Regional Innovation Strategy)* and subregional, such as the draft *Vision for West Cumbria*. The European Structural Funds *Single Programming Document* and *SRB 6 Guidance* are extremely important determinants of action on the ground.

It is far too easy to be flip and critical of these from a sustainability perspective – lowest common denominator "business as usual" approach, lack of focus, critical issues still not on the agenda, and so on.

However, we have come a very long way since the unofficial *North West Partnership Regional Economic Strategy* of 1996 in which environment and social inclusion were token (North West Partnership, 1996). Five years on, sustainable development is now de rigeur as a "defining principle" or "cross-cutting theme".

We have also come a very long way, in terms of process, from top-down exhortation towards more intelligent and interactive engagement and ownership. An exemplar has been the development of the *Regional Strategy*, which was extensively debated. For example, the NWBLT organised no less than 31 industrial sector groups to input ideas. The quality of the process of strategy development is arguably as important as the glossy product.

Finally, the benefits of sustainability appraisals of strategies are now beginning to be understood and, in the next phase of regional strategy development, will become the norm. We have now irrevocably passed the point at which sustainable development is ignored or marginalised in regional strategies. We are at the very beginning of a new phase: beyond active tokenism and towards shaping the agenda.

Ideas into action

How can the well-known forces – inertia, short termism, absence of innovation and vision – that block sustainable development be vaporised? Part of the solution is information and intelligence, advocacy and communications. Here are examples:

"The environment" is still widely perceived, for example by many of those in "economic development'", as a constraint. These people hold that crinkly sheds on greenfield sites, coupled with road improvements, are the solution. On the contrary, the environment is a huge economic asset. *The Environmental Economy of the Northwest Study* – developed by a multi-agency partnership including SNW – marshalled the evidence. (Environment Agency, 2000). The environmental economy of the Northwest accounts for over 100,000 jobs and an annual turnover of £2.96bn – more than the construction sector. At least 48,000 jobs are directly dependent on environmentally-driven tourism.

This evidence-based weaponry is powerful. The study was intended to underline the importance of the emerging environmental technologies and services sector. This was in danger of being overlooked in favour of the established sectors such as chemicals or more obvious sectors such as creative industries. Its impact has helped to ensure that the new cluster – Envirolink North West – is firmly in the Northwest Development Agency's sights and is being actively supported.

Climate change can be sidelined as a remote and long-range problem for national and global attention. For the last three years, the Northwest Climate Group – again a cross-sectoral partnership – has been working on regional scoping studies, a regional greenhouse gas inventory, and a relentless programme of stakeholder engagement, media work and communications. In June 2000, a concerted media blitz around a conference on climate change and tourism, alongside the release of the greenhouse gas inventory, achieved a national and regional press/TV/radio audience reach of 11.7 million! Substantially helped by last year's floods, this is now an "on-the-agenda" topic beginning to inform policy and action.

The Northwest Climate Group has a further role in advocating solutions. Renewable energies have immense triple-bottom-line, win-win-win potential, particularly in areas like the Northwest with its coastline and topography. The environmental benefits include savings in CO_2 emissions; social benefits might include jobs in Merseyside and West Cumbria; economic benefits would accrue to contractors, landowners and local authorities.

National Wind Power's Lambrigg Wind Farm near Kendal, for instance, offsets around 14,000 tonnes of CO_2 per annum, employed 25 local construction workers and provides sufficient electricity to meet the needs of 4,000 homes.

Despite the elegance of renewable energies – wind and biomass in particular – there has been a lack of hard information to counter knee-jerk NIMBYISM. We are currently managing a comprehensive study of the economics and the technologies. In parallel – and importantly – an extensive stakeholder engagement programme is taking place.

In these and many other evidence-based advocacy initiatives, creative communications have been vital. The interface with decision-makers, judicious use of the media, and the continuous infiltration into many regional forums have all been part of the marketing mix. This has been approached on a strictly de-greening basis, and the colour green remains off-limits.

Where do we go from here?

"The amount of wealth extracted from one unit of natural resources can quadruple. Thus we can live twice as well – yet use half as much"

von Weizsacker et al, 1997

Most decision-makers and policy-makers would see Factor Four as a sun cream. Some of the most seriously unsustainable trends such as car use are barely on the regional agenda yet. But, as we have seen, progress is possible. Based on SNW experience, here are some of the ideas on which we – always with partners – are working. They are not blue sky, and assume the likely scenario of a roughly "business as usual" approach in Whitehall:

Capacity building for the professionals

Successful regeneration is complex, challenging and takes time. Many attempts at regeneration fail. There are neighbourhoods in the Northwest which have been the subject of serial regeneration initiatives but remain socially blighted, environmentally degraded and economically written off. It is not enough to hector or lecture the professionals in regional policy, partnerships, regeneration and so on in general terms. Engaging them with sustainability means building their capacity. The Urban Task Force / Urban White Paper proposals for regional centres of excellence in urban regeneration must be shaped to build capacity in sustainable urban (and rural) regeneration.

Leadership development for sustainable regional development

Innovation and creativity – institutional, scientific or industrial – needs leadership. We must develop the sustainable regional development champions of the future through imaginative leadership programmes. It may be true that leadership cannot be taught, but opportunities must be made for the fast stream in all sectors to be exposed to leading-edge sustainability ideas. This is not a question of tacking on "sustainability" to university and HEI courses. It will demand breakthroughs in ways of identifying potential leaders and in supporting their growth.

Regional intelligence and advocacy on climate change

Climate change has become a uniquely powerful stimulus for constructive engagement in sustainable development. We must develop much stronger and better resourced regional centres. These must be built on the partnerships such as the Northwest Climate Group that are coming together in the regions linking into the UK Climate Impacts Programme.

Regional sustainable development organisations

We believe that we have proved that there is a constructive role for regional organisations such as SNW – and others such as Sustainability South West – working with the grain of the regional machinery but independent of government and the regional chambers/ assemblies. As critical friends, their roles should be to challenge as well as to promote solutions. They must be firmly anchored in the partnership sector. They must not degenerate into talking shops.

At the end of the beginning, the challenge of shifting a region of seven million people away from unsustainable trends remains daunting. It is vital that it is approached with enthusiasm, creativity and as a modernising and exciting path. It is not enough to be dull, worthy, correct and sidelined. We must continually remind ourselves of Einstein's insight that *"Today's problems cannot be solved if we continue to think the way we thought when we created them"*.

MARGINS TO MAINSTREAM (2005)

Making sustainable development a reality for the regions

"We know the problems...and we know the solution – sustainable development. The issue is the political will"
Tony Blair, Johannesburg 2/9/2002

In this, the year of the World Summit, the global challenge has become clearer – or less clear, depending on your analysis! We are still waiting for a Prime Ministerial speech with some real substance on sustainable development from a national perspective. At the recent Urban Summit, however, both John Prescott and Gordon Brown spoke out strongly for *"sustainable communities"*. The Chancellor spoke of *"high and stable levels of growth and employment"* and sustainable development. In fact, during the first morning of the Summit, the word "sustainable" was mentioned from the platform 31 times! There are some huge challenges ahead – such as the UK's forthcoming energy policy – a litmus test of the government's commitment. There is evidence of real progress and innovation in leading businesses addressing corporate social responsibility and sustainable development.

Meanwhile, at the local level, the sustainable development operatives at Ian Christie's Fledgling and Three Pylons District Councils agonise over the linkage between LA21, Community Strategies, LSPs and all the other local strategies. So that's all right then!

Well, it's not the whole story. The devolved administrations – in Scotland and Wales at least – seem to be grasping the sustainable development thistle or nettle, and there are encouraging signs of SD being mainstreamed rather than marginalised. But what about sustainable development and the English regions? The regional level is said to be increasingly significant. So what? Who cares? Is progress possible and what does the regional dimension mean for the local?

Picture this – our SD Officer at Three Pylons District Council has been emailed – flagged urgent – by the economic development heavy squad in the Chief Executive's Department. The task is to put an SD spin on the megabid the rugger buggers in Econ Dev are concocting for their inward investment site bid to Up Middle England (UME) Development Agency. A "guiding principle" – for UME in disbursing its cash is "contributing to sustainable development". The site will of course result in further crinkly sheds in greenfields and the associated contributions to unsustainable development that are too obvious to rehearse here. Where to begin? *Regional Planning Guidance? The Regional Economic Strategy? The Regional Sustainable Development Framework?* All three, or something else, or what?

Many commentators have pointed out (in, for example, the IPPR report) that the regional structures are complex, conflicting and were not designed to deliver sustainable development. The White Paper on the English Regions articulates the need for an *"overarching strategy"*, which will act as *"the sustainable development framework for the region, replacing the voluntary frameworks"*.

But who can predict the pace of serious regional devolution following referenda? As Martin Burch points out, *"There is not yet any indication of widespread public enthusiasm for an elected body"*. And he is writing about the Northwest, widely regarded as one of the leaders in regional devolution. There are confusing signs that the core cities concept may be gathering force as a very different way of devolving governance from Whitehall, but to cities, not regions.

And then there is public opinion. DEFRA's most recent magisterial survey encouragingly concludes that *"Almost all respondents had heard of climate change, global warming or the greenhouse effect"* but discouragingly concludes that *"There was much less awareness of environmental campaigns and concepts such as sustainable development"* and very discouragingly concludes that *"Awareness had not changed significantly since 1996/97".*

In the absence of joined-up regional structures and clear leadership, there is huge inertia in the public sector and last – but by no means least – public opinion. Is there any evidence that the regional level can be a positive driver of sustainable development – the bridge between the local and the national/international?

Well, there have been material achievements over the last decade that could only have been achieved through effective joining-up of the national, regional and local with shared objectives. Take the Mersey Basin Campaign for instance, established in 1985: a twenty-five year campaign to improve water quality across the entire catchment, stimulate waterside regeneration, and engage communities – and businesses – in the process. The results, across a river catchment of six million people, transcended local authority boundaries: research commissioned by the Campaign showed that the value of previously undevelopable brownfield waterside sites increased by some 40 per cent with water quality improvements. There are vivid and compelling examples to prove the point. Salford Quays, at its lowest ebb, had negative land value and was incapable of being offloaded to any developer. Now the locus for the Lowry, the Imperial War Museum and residential, office and retail development, what is now described as "Manchester's Waterfront" is a vibrant and thriving regional asset.

How was this substantial progress in the direction of sustainable development possible? Intelligent national decision-making by OFWAT enabled massive investment in water quality improvements linked to regional leadership of the Campaign and a very strong partnership including the water company (United Utilities), The Environment Agency, leading corporates, and local authorities with a shared agenda. This national and regional action connects through to local action on the ground co-ordinated by locally-managed Campaign River Valley Initiatives. There are similar stories in other regions and the evidence of real progress is beyond doubt.

In the run-up to WSSD, a group of us in the Northwest decided to try to make the connection between the challenge of raising awareness of sustainable development in the region, and WSSD, by highlighting tangible examples of success, excellence, and achievement. *IE (Industrial Evolution)* was born – an attempt to highlight the positives and excite the disenchanted but interested. The publication ranges over the big issues including climate change, regeneration and social entrepreneurship, as well as business responses to sustainable development. The central theme is that of "margins to mainstream", reflecting and echoing the Sustainable Development Commission's firm belief that sustainable development must be nothing less than the central organising principle and not, repeat not, an add-on to business as usual. *IE* paints a vivid and compelling picture of real progress being made in the Northwest, in spite of the complexity and contradictions of regional structures.

So where does this leave our struggling Sustainable Development Officer at Three Pylons D.C. faced with mission impossible?

Firstly, forget about Local Agenda 21. It is a badge that no longer adds any value or sets the spirits racing. I didn't hear LA21 mentioned in two days at the Urban Summit. The new vocabulary is that of "sustainable communities" and the new mechanisms are, of course, LSPs and Community Plans.

Secondly, a valuable technique to master is that of sustainability appraisal – increasingly being used in funding regimes and a way of attempting to influence the worst excesses of hardcore "economic development".

Thirdly, the regional agenda is important. Getting to grips with and trying to contribute to the growing mountain of strategies and action plans does matter.

And finally, Tony Blair is quite right – political will is vital and leadership is the key. In analysing the critical success factors that propel organisations – whether regional bodies, companies, local authorities, NGOs or community groups – towards sustainable development, the single and by far the most powerful dimension is leadership. And leadership can be found in the most surprising places! Even, perhaps, one day in Three Pylons District Council.

MANCHESTER IS THE NEW VENICE (2006)

Our cities are reviving. But there are big differences between the economic performance of London and the South East and the rest of the country. When the UK as a whole can only rate 108th on the *Happy Planet Index*, is the rediscovery of city regions missing the point?

It's grim down south. The economy is overheating. House prices defeat average earners who are forced to commute farther than anywhere else in Europe. This summer saw a water crisis. SUVs in Surbiton remained unwashed. The heatwave created desperate conditions in the Underground. The terrorism threat brought fear and loathing to the airports. City slickers pocketed bonuses that exceeded the entire UK transport budget. Pockets of poverty in London shamefully topped the government's own league tables. A Mad Max future beckons.

It's cool up north. Forests of cranes in the northern city centres and the decreasing rate of bankruptcy of hair salons signal economic revival. Heavy industry, manufacturing and the resulting environmental degradation are being replaced by the knowledge economy. Unemployment has plummeted. Fewer people leave the core cities: Birmingham, Bristol, Leeds, Liverpool, Manchester, Newcastle, Nottingham and Sheffield City centres are being repopulated. Between 1990 and 2005 the population of city-centre Manchester grew from 1000 to 15000. Crime rates are falling. Educational attainment is improving. Decades of decline are being reversed. A golden age is just round the corner.

Analyses such as Michael Parkinson's magisterial *"State of the English Cities Report"* confirm this northern urban renaissance. There are big differences between our regions on a crude comparative basis. GDP per capita in 2002 varied between £27,000 in London and £13,000 in the North East.

But these figures do not reveal the huge differences in life chances between the rich and poor places within regions. Ten years' difference in life expectancy is a disgrace to a civilised society. Nothing new here, you might say. Throughout history, cities have risen and fallen. They have always been the crucibles of economic growth, culture and innovation. Think of Florence under the Medicis or Edinburgh in the Age of Enlightenment. Think of successful European cities today – Milan or Stuttgart have a far higher GDP per capita than the English regions outside London and the South East.

Following the spectacular popular rejection of the referendum in the North East in November 2004, the possibility of elected regional government in England disappeared for a generation. So, hey presto! Out of the policy wonkery hat was pulled the twitching rabbit of city regions – the concept that local economies do not acknowledge arcane local authority boundaries. For example, to the councillors of both cities, the River Irwell may seem like a demilitarised zone between Manchester and Salford. But both are part of a wider city region including towns in leafy, greenbelt Cheshire. From a sustainability perspective it is blindingly obvious that climate change, storms, floods, rivers, drug dealing and traffic gridlock do not recognise lines on maps. People know this. The successful *Manchester is My Planet* climate change campaign has caught the public imagination over a wide area. More than 15,000 people have pledged to act.

The Treasury talks of lifting the economic performance of cities. The Local Government Association pays lip service to sustainable development in its examination of *"City Regions and Beyond"*. There is talk of double devolution and elected mayors. But the entire city regions debate is shaped by the discredited notion that the comparative economic performance of city regions is what counts: why can't Liverpool have the GDP per capita of Barcelona?

The ever-enterprising New Economics Foundation launched the *Happy Planet Index* in July. This was the first index to combine environmental impact with well-being to measure the environmental efficiency with which countries provide long and happy lives. The results are shocking – the UK is a poor 108th, just below Libya but above Laos. The UK's heavy ecological impact is to blame. If everyone in the world consumed as we do in the UK we would need 3.1 planet Earths to support us. Significantly, Germany's ecological footprint is twice as efficient as the USA at generating long, happy lives based on the resources consumed. Being smarter and greener does not mean a return to a mythical pre-industrial state of grace.

The delusion that the economies, the societies and the environments of our very different city regions must be driven towards GDP convergence is undesirable and unrealistic. Stalin never succeeded. Castro struggled. The debate must move on: the North is not the South. Bolton is not Basingstoke. Good! The great urbanist Jane Jacobs wrote: *"While Addis Ababa was dying, Rome was rising. While the great cities of China were stagnating, Venice was rising. No doubt in future (provided of course there is a future for a world booby-trapped by nuclear weapons) people will remark that while the cities of Great Britain were dying, those of Japan were rising."* She wrote that in 1984. Neither she nor anyone else could have foreseen that our cities would revive. Who can say which of them will successfully adapt to the imperative of climate change and a low-carbon future?

Continuous built-up areas, their subsidiary centres and suburbs and satellite towns and rural hinterlands are interconnected. Their problems are interconnected. So are their economies and their people. City regions have the potential of smart solutions for their sustainable development. Manchester is the new Venice.

ENGLAND'S NORTHWEST: OVER BUT NOT OUT
(2011)

Flashback to the early, heady days of New Labour and The Northwest Project. July 1997: Windermere, shimmering in the summer sunshine. Conference delegates ducked as the Red Arrows screamed overhead. Newly-elected Deputy Prime Minister John Prescott had just energised us with his decision that Cumbria was definitively in our region. The long march towards regional devolution had begun.

Flash forward to the day the music died: 26th July 2010, the Northwest Development Agency's list of projects and initiatives to be axed. The NWDA cash machine had been ram-raided and emptied by the Maoist (their word) Coalition storm-troopers.

Who killed the regional project?
- The bankers and financiers who trashed the economy, opening the door to the Coalition's cuts?
- Whitehall – dysfunctional and parochial, patronising the regions as recalcitrant colonies?
- New Labour – dirigiste and deeply conservative?
- The people of the North East and their spectacular "No" vote in the first – and inevitably last – regional referendum?
- False gods – the delusion that progress can be measured by GDP, and that the highest goal of civilisation is "closing the productivity gap" with London and the South East?
- The Northwest Regional Assembly – strangled with strategies; achingly boring and ignored?
- The failure of the region's sustainable development fraternity (including myself) to destroy the false gods and articulate a more compelling path to a better future?

All of us?

Lasting achievements?
Ours was the first region in the world to industrialise on a massive scale. For a time, we really believed that we were leading the transformation to a new, sustainable industrial evolution. Sustainability Northwest showed the power of ideas, innovation and action – the first regional climate change impacts work, the first attempt at regional carbon counting, the first environmental technologies cluster (Envirolink), the first serious environmental business support agency in the UK (Enworks) and much more – about a decade ahead of "mainstreaming". And we welcomed the Northwest Development Agency – a focus for the region, the sponsor of many flagship projects, and often courageous, in spite of the blizzard of absurd targets raining down from Whitehall.

What have we learned from the crusade for sustainable regional development?
We know that there is no serious alternative to the coherence of the idea of sustainable development. The global scale matters for our survival. Local matters – people care passionately about their home, street, neighbourhood. And the regional scale made sense for so much – planning, environment and landscape, transport, energy, river basin management and yes – many dimensions of "economic development". But our endless strategising and agonising over indicators was a wasteful diversion. In the real world, shopping remained the zeitgeist. The saddest monument to this period is tin "retail parks" with their dismal acres of parking . And we know for sure that one size does not fit all – the Northwest is not the South West – dirigisme has failed in the past and will surely fail in the future.

Was the regional project in the Northwest an expensive cul-de-sac? Or was its failure a liberating step on the road to the big society, localism, power to the people and sustainable development?

English Regionalism is over for at least a generation. But pockets of enlightenment remain – in the universities, business and the third sector. Could this heady mix of business/localism/anarchism lead us towards sustainable development? For the sake of future generations, let's hope so.

4 PARTNERSHIP – THE AEROSOL WORD

Partnership "the aerosol word" – sprayed on everything, means nothing. It's too easy to be cynical about partnership working. The Northwest…more visions than Mother Theresa; more pilots than the RAF; more partnerships than… but this type of thinking gets you nowhere. Our region has been a fertile test bed for experiment, innovation and real achievement in cross-sectoral partnership working in pursuit of better places.

I began to be exposed to this with MIH in Liverpool in the darkest days of the city's decline – late seventies / early eighties. MIH (Now Riverside) was a dynamic and enterprising housing association always keen to be in the lead. I was its Special Projects Manager, in at the deep end with housing co-operatives in some of the most deprived places in Britain. It was clear to me that the kind of partnership working that was essential for co-ops and community projects to thrive was infinitely superior to the Stalinism and dictat of Militant. They helped to bring Liverpool to its knees. An unintended consequence, though, was the post-riots appearance of Michael Heseltine (then Secretary of State for The Environment), the godfather of innovation in partnership initiatives that were to form a big part of my professional future.

Fast forward: SPRAY IT AGAIN was a 2007 column for *Place North West* inspired by the North Korean possibilities of Gordon Brown's impending premiership.

LINKING TOWN WITH COUNTRY recalls my early experience with Groundwork in Macclesfield. The first

Groundwork strapline *"Partnership for Action"* (1983), like the Groundwork movement itself, was years ahead of its time. There's no doubt that Groundwork was a significant pioneer of cross-sectoral partnership working. This piece was a contribution to the book *Partnership for action – Groundwork: the early years* that I co-edited with Phil Barton, published in 2012.

STICKING UP FOR PARTNERSHIP was a short rant for *Guardian Public* in 2007. The partnership idea remained novel to some people, even then.

Remarkably little considered writing about partnership working has been penned by experienced practitioners of its dark arts. I've made several attempts at putting this right. PARTNERSHIP: NO ONE SAID IT WOULD BE EASY for *Town Planning Review* summarised the critical success factors for the Mersey Basin Campaign as it came to an end in 2010. I like to think of MBC as an exemplar partnership that married strategic thought leadership and local project delivery in a unique way.

SPRAY IT AGAIN (2007)

Heard the one about the aerosol word?
Partnerships. Sprayed on everything. Means nothing. Practitioners of the black arts of partnership working know what it means, really. A partnership is a loose collection of organisations with conflicting interests, united by mutual loathing, held shakily together in the hope of public money.

That can't be serious?
Partnerships are deeply wonderful...the answer to everything...simply no better alternative...the best way forward...the holy grail of modern life.

What partnerships?
You name it, somebody has set up a partnership for it. From A – alcohol reduction partnerships through L – Local Strategic Partnerships to Z – zoo development partnerships. Then there are partnerships for places: Piccadilly Partnership in Manchester; Ropewalks Partnership in Liverpool; West Cumbria Sheep Bloggers Partnership. The North West Partnership was for the whole region.

Who's in these partnerships?
In development and regeneration, smart partnerships aim to be "cross-sectoral". This means sprinkling private sector stardust over the boredom. Easier said than done. Public sector types think that the private sector "partners" are driven only by greed and that they get paid more too. Private sector "partners" find that the idlers in the public sector can't see past endless meetings. These always lead to more meetings and, on bad days, sub-committees. The voluntary and community "partners" believe that they occupy the moral high ground. Secretly, they enjoy the sandwiches and enjoy scoring a few hits on the suits.

Who's in charge?
I've not enough space for a PhD thesis on the leadership of partnerships! As an officer from a local authority towards the Stalinist end of the spectrum memorably said: *"Glad we've finally got this partnership up and running...just remember one thing: you can do anything you like as long as it's exactly what we want you to do"*. Seriously, though, successful partnerships need strong leadership.

Why bother?
It's like this: everything is connected. A beautiful butterfly flapping her wings as she flits around Beatrix Potter's garden sets off a chain of events that results in a pie being eaten in Wigan. One world. Cue magnificent sunsets. Trumpets toot. In practice, though, many things seem disconnected, chaotic and confusing. As the great T L DeWinne pointed out *"The end of civilisation as we know it will not be brought about by nuclear holocaust or terrorist outage but by bumbling bureaucracy"*. See for yourself...a new game, fun for all the office, is logo-hunting. The rules are simple. The winner, within an agreed time, say 24 hours, spots the report / site sign / notepaper / whatever with the highest logo count. Scary, you will find.

Isn't this just waffle of the worst kind?
No. Successful partnerships save time and money and achieve more with less.

Does everything need to be a partnership?
Well, there are people who worry, the moment they crawl out of bed, that their day will be empty without a partnership meeting or board to attend. But the answer is no. We don't need to form partnerships to go to the lavatory. Partnerships should be created when they are needed.

And the next big thing in the world of partnerships?
What about partnerships in the brave new morning of Broon's Britain? Will the unreconstructed enemies of partnerships and advocates of the North Korean way step forward from the shadows? Will Sir Humphrey really devolve power to local authorities? Will development really speed up? Will everything be so joined up and elegant that we won't need partnerships? In your dreams. Experienced partners know that if you're not at the table, you're on the menu.

LINKING TOWN WITH COUNTRY (2012)

Groundwork in Macclesfield

It was a dark and stormy night, the week before Christmas 1983. The suited – and booted – dignitaries of Macclesfield were crammed into Bollington Town Hall enjoying a civilised festive drink to celebrate the first few months of Groundwork in Macclesfield. The lights of the civic Christmas tree winked cheerily outside. With a crash, the door was flung open and a torrent of tiny Brownies screeched in and headed straight for the crisps and canapes. Nobody had remembered that it was Brownie night. I knew at the time that this was some kind of metaphor, but what might it mean?

People

When I left MIH in Liverpool, my boss, the legendary Barry Natton, ominously warned: *"You'll see, it's lonely at the top"*. This turned out to be completely wrong. There was W G B "Bill" Grant, the revered founder-chair of Groundwork Macclesfield. A retired Ciba-Geigy Clayton MD, he knew everybody and everything and was a priceless sounding board for me. Bill was the perfect non-executive: worldly, astute, never issuing instructions, somehow guiding me to come to the right decision myself. Bill was later to play a very significant role nationally on the Groundwork Foundation board.

There was John Davidson with, the others at the Groundwork Northwest Development Unit. I had harboured doubts about whether leaving a good career in an exciting housing association to join something as uncertain, experimental and flaky as Groundwork would be a smart move. I vividly remember the moment when I knew

I had done the right thing. It was a coffee, and chat, at The Royal Exchange in Manchester with John Davidson and his wife Joan – then, I think, beginning research for what was to become *"How Green is Your City?"*. The penny dropped – we were changing the world from the bottom up! Local to global! John and Joan were a compelling and charismatic double act.

And then there were the other Northwest Groundwork Trust Executive Directors. I can't begin to find the right adjective to sum up this diverse gang – some of us are still friends today. Whatever else, our early gatherings in the Countryside Commission's tatty offices in Deansgate were never, ever boring.

Government Office North West blew apart stereotypical notions of civil servants as obstructive timeservers. Nothing could have been further from the truth. It was their Ralph Porteous – a member of my board – who first described Groundwork as *"this great movement of ours"*. It was their Ian Jamieson who brilliantly averted Whitehall from blocking "creative" uses of Derelict Land Grant. *"I must have been pissed when I agreed to that"*, he would quip.

And above all, central to the success of our efforts the staff – a tiny, professional "core staff" on reasonable salaries with a constantly shifting mix of secondees from ICI, British Gas and poorly-paid young people on Manpower Services Commission temporary employment schemes.

Was everybody connected to this innovative new world of Groundwork with us? No. There were remnant cases of "can't do" functionaries who felt threatened and would have been happier sticking with business as usual. There was no shortage of imperfect moments.

The lesson that I took from this – people are far far more important than organisational structures, and "can-do" people refuse to be crushed and often achieve wonders.

Place

Macclesfield Borough formed the southern fringe of Greater Manchester – a "green lung for the city" was one way of looking at it...more than 200 square miles; headquartered in former silk town Macclesfield, small towns such as Knutsford, commuter centres like Wilmslow, many villages, and a large rural hinterland.

I was mistaken in expecting this to be a total contrast to the chaos of Liverpool and that the citizens would be less disunited. The very first week as Trust Executive Director I was disabused of such nonsense. Having struggled to set up David Wilcox's twin carousel projector gear at a meeting of Bollington Town Council, I relaxed, expecting them to enjoy the Groundwork propaganda. But I was shaken by the vitriolic attacks on the Stalinist Borough Council (headquartered three miles away). Many of the town councillors had not recovered from local government reorganisation in 1974. I later came to appreciate the pride, bolshiness and distinctiveness of small places – like Bollington – where I still live.

Lesson from this – administrative boundaries are meaningless in the real world – pride of place and enmity are two sides of the same coin.

Planning

In spite of the sleepy-hollow default mode of Macclesfield Borough Council, there was serious Groundwork action by the time I got there. One of the lasting legacies of Groundwork local authority funding is The Middlewood Way – a 16km traffic-free greenway from Macclesfield to Marple. This runs parallel to the Macclesfield Canal – early Groundwork interventions here were 21km of towpath improvements using MSC labour. Up to 80 people were involved. MSC "schemes" were to become a major source of labour for Groundwork projects across the Northwest.

We conceptualised our early work in three strands:
- Improving access to the countryside (projects ranged from publishing guide books, to landscaping car parks, to setting up cycle hire facilities)
- Environmental improvement (from reclamation of derelict land for leisure, to landscaping around former mills to enhance the prospects of attracting tenants and encouraging investment)
- Property and land development (notably the trust's own visitor centre and offices in Bollington and the heritage centre in Knutsford).

In practice, we were strategy-lite. Very little time was spent on elaborate plans. We were opportunistic and responsive. Chance favoured the prepared mind, we believed. Many projects were brought to us. We started our adventures as publisher of local guides when we were presented with the draft of an excellent cycling guide to the area. Our extensive involvement in the area of the Adelphi Mill, including woodland acquisition, restoring the derelict gate lodge and award-winning environmental improvements, followed on from a chance encounter with the developer. A local entrepreneur, he was getting no encouragement or help from anyone else.

Our strategy-lite mode was unsettling to the Whitehall machine. An alarming visit from distinguished mandarin Sir George Moseley, Permanent Secretary at The Department of the Environment, culminated – when he was really pressed to express a view – with his one-word summary: *"Interesting"*. Damned with faint praise!

Lesson from this – long after the strategies and plans have been lost, binned and forgotten, the projects remain.

Partnership

Groundwork Macclesfield's second annual report (1983-84) was headlined *"Partnerships"*. We attempted to explain what this meant in practice by focusing on one area and how we were *"Fitting the jigsaw together"*. Alongside a map, 10 projects were illustrated and captioned-The Middlewood Way (greenway); our own cycle hire enterprise; environmental improvements to a small commercial haulage site; a car park for Adelphi Mill businesses and visitors to The Macclesfield Canal; the Canal towpath; our visitor centre; a semi-derelict wharf; a remnant woodland that we had acquired; and a derelict goods yard.

The point was that partnership working was the only way. There was no alternative. All of these projects interlocked and benefited each other. But no single organisation was responsible. There were multiple ownerships, interests, objectives, financial stakes, funding possibilities and local impacts. Here was an exemplar of how Groundwork could bring it all together, as honest broker, working in partnership with the public, private and voluntary sectors as well as local people.

It may seem extraordinary to some today that this was innovative, radical, and subverted the natural order of things. It was particularly taxing for the public sector. A typical instance was a negotiation with British Waterways. BW was so shaken with the idea that we might implement environmental improvements on what they regarded as "their" land that on one site visit they fielded no less than seven people. There were only two of us. We were undeterred by their blockbuster approach and won through in the end.

Lesson from this – it is easier said than done, but partnership working can make 1+1 = 3: better together.

Groundwork Macclesfield went on to become

Groundwork Macclesfield and Vale Royal – the first trust in the growing Groundwork network to expand its geographical coverage. This presented a new dimension of "challenges" as well as opportunities. Then there was evolution into into Groundwork Cheshire. Now, in 2012, I believe that further expansion is being considered.

Was it all worth it? That was for others at the time to judge. Was it worth it for me? Yes, it was a great privilege being able to set up and lead what would now be described as a social enterprise – an integral part of the embryonic *"great movement of ours"*. No regrets. Deja vu – The Macclesfield Canal is back in my life and I can sense a government youth unemployment scheme just waiting round the next corner.

As for the Brownies, I'm still not sure of the answer.

STICKING UP FOR PARTNERSHIP (2007)

People may be heartily sick of hearing the P-word, but we still haven't got enough of it.

"Partnership" is an aerosol word – sprayed on everything, but meaning absolutely nothing. In practice it amounts to no more than a loose collection of people with conflicting interests, united by mutual loathing, held together only by the prospect of securing government funny money. The best way to destroy the opposition is to make them your partner. Only joking – that rant was an attempt to make the point that there are, of course, people with bad experiences of partnerships. It's also true that over the last 20 years, the P-word has been abused and overused.

Anyone who crosses the public/private demilitarised zone knows that stereotypical views of the other side are commonplace.

It is difficult to climb out of bunkers. But serious partnerships can add up to much more than the sum of the parts. People and places do benefit from joined-up rather than chaotic and conflicting initiatives and services.

Yet the partnership sector is strangely reticent. Who speaks up for partnerships? The sector remains dispersed and disconnected – from itself! But there is no going back. In a landscape littered with the disastrous debris of yesterday's thinking, partnership surely is an idea whose time has come.

PARTNERSHIP: NO ONE SAID IT WOULD BE EASY
(2010)

"Partnership" has been described as the aerosol word – sprayed on everything, means nothing. It has entered the Local Government Association (LGA) magisterial list of *"Top 100 non-words"* alongside atrocities such as "beaconicity" and "peer challenge" (LGA, 2007). The Dictionary of Urbanism quips: *"Partnership: a loose connection of people and organisations with conflicting interests held together by the prospect of securing government money"* (Cowan, 2005). One of my early partnership baptisms was establishing a Groundwork Trust with one of our more Stalinist local authorities. *"Just remember one thing"* a world-weary senior officer lectured me *"...we're totally signed up to this partnership...so long as you stick to doing exactly what we want"*.

How do we make better places? "Partnership" is the mantra. But what are partnerships, and how can they be made to work? Are there special ingredients in successful partnerships? How do we improve their design, development and leadership?

Is the LGA's reductive definition of partnership as "working together" adequate? No. Our economy, society and environment are dysfunctional. The sky is dark with black swans coming home to roost. Apocalyptic visions encircle. Climate change is inexorable. Our economy has experienced a spectacular episode of value destruction. Inequalities shame us (Wilkinson and Pickett, 2010).

Partnerships for sustainable development

This toxic state of affairs confirms that there is no alternative to the organising principle of sustainable development. Business as usual is not a viable option. Sustainable development means dismantling unnecessary sectoral and institutional barriers. New links and alliances must be forged. Partnerships are useful. Partnership working can contribute to the future of the planet and society. More must be achieved with less. Rocky Mountain Institute's Amory Lovins: *"Over the next decade our species takes its university finals. Get revising."* (Lovins et al., 1998). And that was more than ten years ago.

Partnerships are not the answer to everything. But there is compelling evidence that the whole can be made to add up to very much more than the sum of the parts. The Mersey Basin Campaign is an excellent example (Mersey Basin Campaign, 2010).

Partnerships in practice

To appreciate the present state of partnership practice in the UK public sector, it is helpful to remember its origins. Ecology and biology illuminate species interdependence and symbiosis. A fast rewind to the early nineteen-eighties is more directly relevant to planners: several drivers then combined to fire the starting pistol on the regeneration partnerships bandwagon. Top-down Thatcherite rhetoric waxed lyrical about rolling back the boundaries of the state and privatisation of public assets. Bottom-up community action, conflict and partnerships were capturing the attention of the media. The 1981 Toxteth riots, the worst in mainland Britain for a century, were a landmark. Michael Heseltine, Thatcher's Secretary of State for the Environment, parachuted into Liverpool in their wake (Unger, 2007). Heseltine vividly recounted his experiences at the Mersey Basin Campaign's final conference in 2009 under the title *"It took a riot"*.

Heseltine redirected Groundwork from what would have been a dreary public sector experiment into the first government-backed regeneration partnership. Its first strap line was *"Partnerships for action"*. He initiated the Mersey Basin Campaign as an unprecedented 25-year programme. The common factors in these and other emerging initiatives were innovation, action and partnership across the sectors. Business leadership was thought to be a magic ingredient, sprinkling stardust.

A huge volume of water has flowed under the bridges of the Mersey as well as less interesting and provocative rivers since then. The concept of partnership working has shifted from the margins to the mainstream of public policy and delivery in central government, government agencies and local government. There are people who can barely get out of bed without the thought of a partnership meeting to attend.

But the exponential growth in partnership working and partnership organisations has not eradicated the deep-rooted cultural differences and suspicions between the sectors. Crude snapshots: the public sector is "rights driven", the private sector is "profits driven" and the voluntary sector is "values driven". But these stereotypes are becoming meaningless. Boundaries are blurred. Charities trade, businesses dabble in "corporate responsibility" and the public sector enables and contracts. Each adopts the language of the others. Depressingly, all refer to "people" as "customers". One consequence has been the emergence – from these shifting sands – of intermediary bodies. Many are constructed as partnerships spanning the public/private/voluntary divides.

Types of partnership

There are innumerable types of partnership operating at every spatial level from global strategy through to the neighbourhood delivery of essential services. Some are official. Others are bottom-up. Some are area-based; others are thematic. Some command powers and resources; others are flaccid talking shops. There is no universally applicable definition. The International Business Leaders Forum (IBLF) with the Cambridge Programme for Industry has been working for years on partnership research and capacity building: *"Partnership is a cross-sectoral alliance in which individuals, groups or organisations agree to work together to fulfil obligations or undertake a specific task; to share the risks as well as the benefits; and review the relationship regularly, revising their agreement as necessary"* (Tennyson, 1998).

This definition fails to capture the chemistry, synergy and added value of unconventional alliances. Partnership theory remains sketchy. It is a Cinderella area of research despite its potential:

"Open and collaborative models of organisation will increasingly trump closed and hierarchical models as a way to promote innovation, organise work and engage consumers" (Leadbeater, 2008).

Critical success factors for partnerships

What are the critical success factors for partnership working?

Partnerships need leadership

There must be an unambiguous answer to the "Take me to the person in charge!" demand. Leadership can emerge and manifest itself in many ways. It may be formally bestowed (by appointment or election) or it may be unofficial. You know it when you see it. For a partnership to be more than a therapeutic talking shop, there must be leadership and direction. This need not demean the contributions of all partners. A strong partnership leader will keep the partnership intact and maintain momentum through setbacks and controversies. And he will know when the moment for decisiveness arrives.

Partnerships need a shared vision

It may be ambitious; bold; long term. But it must be crystal clear. "The return of fish to the Mersey" is a classic example. A multiple bullet-point waffle of LGA non-words is not. The words "world-class", "community" or "economic development" are always suspect. Blurring of vision and mission-drift in the pursuit of funding must be resisted.

People are more important than structures

Progress is more important than bureaucratic process. And organisational construction and destruction can be a huge diversion. Many in the public sector excite themselves with deckchair rearrangement. Others are overwhelmed with target compliance and the creaking machinery of government: *"The end of civilisation as we know it will not be brought about by nuclear holocaust or terrorist outrage but by bumbling bureaucracy"* (de Winne, 2010).

The best partnership people trust their judgement rather than box ticking "toolkits" or lowest-common-denominator "guidance" imposed by Whitehall. They take risks and make a difference.

Business is part of the solution

By definition, cross-sectoral partnerships include business. Those hardened by experience in the partnership front line know that the "public sector bad; private sector good" mantra is absurd. The reverse claim is equally absurd. There are few more excruciating sights than a captain of industry used to leading, keen to make decisions, anxious to get results, parachuted into a mainly public sector board and quickly lost – as if in a foreign country, unable to speak the language, without a map. The best learn quickly and bring valuable insights. In progressive, successful companies, innovation is in the DNA. There is immense potential for innovation in the public sector and in partnerships.

Partnerships need values
They need a unifying idea. There must be a coherent foundation on which strategy, delivery, and priorities can be built. There are countless examples of flawed ideas on which flaky partnerships are constructed particularly in the discredited area of "local economic development". Many have yet to accept that the plane has crashed, that there must be a higher ambition than increasing Gross Value Added despite the mountain of evidence that this is a perverted measure of the health of a region or city. It would be comforting if the worldwide economic chaos and the threat of catastrophic climate change fused so as to wipe out these false gods. It would be heartening to believe that the partnerships seriously committed to sustainable development would be the survivors. Unhappily, it would be naiive.

Partnerships should be designed with realistic timescales
The Mersey Basin Campaign was designed with a 25-year life. This, though exceptional, turned out to be about right. Different timescales often fail to synchronise. There is geological time – we tend not to dwell on the fact that we are the ashes of long-dead stars. There is community time – one measure is the length of a childhood. There is government initiative time – typically quick-fix, three or at best five years; here today, gone tomorrow. There is ecological time – we now know that this can be frighteningly fast.

Governance matters
In a democracy there is always the question of legitimacy. Few but the most politically aware and correct fret about membership, representation and legitimacy if partnerships deliver uncontroversial and beneficial results. When the balloon goes up and controversy rages, questions of legitimacy arise. "Who elected you? Who do you represent?"

deserves an answer. This may not be easy for cross-sectoral partnerships even in the default position of token elected councillors on the board. Partnership governance must at the very least be transparent.

Partnerships need resources

These may be money, time, knowledge, connections or the ability to influence change. More often than not, a partnership needs a combination of these. The creative shaking of resource cocktails is where the voluntary sector has much to offer. Doing more with less, gearing cash, and corralling people's time – this is meat and potatoes to voluntary organisations and NGOs. And size may not matter as much as might be expected: *"If you think that small things can't make a difference, you've never been to bed with a flea"* (Anon).

Partnerships need to deliver

There must be tangible results. What would you show the international (or extraterrestrial) visitor? Where would they be taken? Who would they meet? You can't take a visitor to a strategy. Strategising is not enough. For years I have quipped that England's Northwest has more visions than Mother Theresa. This is truer than ever: the strategy count is now off the scale. Partnership credibility correlates directly to tangible achievement on the ground.

Partnerships must develop ways of working that are fit for purpose

If the public sector alone is adequate for the task – regulation, legitimacy and so on – there is no need for a partnership. Alternatively, if the private or voluntary sectors can deliver, the partnership is superfluous. How can a partnership achieve more; add real value? There are as many answers as there are successful partnerships. One example from Mersey

Basin Campaign experience is the ability to mediate – without financial or reputational axes to grind, without powers of any kind – bringing conflicting interests quietly and calmly together.

Partnerships must be professional

The quality of their work must be at least as good as the most capable partner. It is not sufficient to be passionate, committed and right. Professionalism in partnership leadership and management is not about self-interest or the erection of defensive barriers of acronyms and jargon. It is about quality in stakeholder relationships and management, building confidence and trust.

Partnerships must communicate

In our multi-media, multi-channel 24-7 communications world with social media expanding exponentially, smart communication is essential. Those who fail to be proactive in communications will be communicated against. They have only themselves to blame. Old models of information and intelligence transmission are redundant. Video killed the radio star. The interactivity of Web 2 is wiping out public sector monologues. Wikipedia gets more traffic than the BBC:

"Web 2 brings back to life more communal and collaborative ways of working which were sidelined by industrial organisation in the twentieth century" (Leadbeater, 1998).

This revolution presents thrilling possibilities for innovation and creativity. Sammy, the Mersey Basin Campaign's celebrity salmon, has blogged across the world.

Where do we go from here?

There is a growing body of experience in the art of cross-sectoral partnership working. Some of the most instructive lessons come from the failures. Like any other mechanism or approach, partnerships are at risk of manipulation and destruction by the cynical and unscrupulous. Time, energy and money may be wasted. Attention can be diverted from pressing and important business. Failed partnerships can leave innocent casualties on the battlefield.

Is the school of hard knocks or the university of life the only response? No. Here are some thoughts:

Whitehall: the policy makers of the future must be savvy in the arts of partnership policy, leadership and development. An immediate priority should be to ensure that all civil service fast streamers are introduced to partnership theory and practice. Their early experience should include exposure to regional or local level partnerships.

Local authorities: it has been estimated that there are more members of partnership boards in the UK than there are elected councillors. Partnership board work is more demanding than council cabinet work. National and local government machinery should commit to building the capacity of elected members so that they can contribute effectively. Parochialism and ignorance are enemies and it is not good enough to be defeatist.

Academics: there has never been a better time than after the crash to explore alternative organisational and management models. The business schools and public sector management researchers in our universities should seriously address the theory and practice of cross-sectoral partnerships. There will be plenty of intellectual capacity when it is finally recognised that local economic development is best ignored.

Partnership leaders (both non-executive and executive): take heart! You are not alone. Above all else, refuse to suffer in silence the bored board. We are all capable of change and learning from others. Reinvention of the wheel is not inevitable. Seeing is believing. *"The best way to destroy the opposition is to make them your partner,"* a private sector non-executive once wisely advised me in my role as a partnership chief executive. My experience has confirmed that he was right.

In messy and cluttered institutional landscapes, successful organisations – and partnerships are no exception – occupy clear positions. Successful partnerships are quick to adapt to changing institutional landscapes while maintaining their focus. Some – like the Mersey Basin Campaign – decide when and how to time their exit in the best interests of their mission. Whether steeped in or dabbling on the edges of partnerships, it is as well to remember the blindingly obvious: if you're not at the table, you're on the menu.

5 WHITEWASHING THE YARD: REGENERATION

Urban regeneration is difficult. Far too many places have been serially regenerated – some of them three or more times since the sixties – and remain impoverished and degraded, a blight on our society. Regeneration should begin with simple steps. Patrick Geddes was right to argue that it begins with whitewashing the back yard. Easier said than done, as I first discovered in 1976 as Michell and Partners' job architect on Eastleigh's General Improvement Area. Our public participation efforts had failed to pick up that under no circumstances could prized racing pigeons be disturbed during the planned back alley improvement works. This led to huge fuss, contract delays, extra costs and a lesson that I was never to forget.

Fast forward to the heights of the Northwest Regional Project. EVERYTHING YOU WANTED TO KNOW ABOUT REGENERATION was a tongue-in-cheek column for *Place North West* in 2007 taking a pop at the burgeoning regeneration industry.

I was co-editor of the first – and last – edition of *Urban Design Forum* (1978) – a bizarre example of self-publishing (and printing) with friends at the exciting – and unorthodox – Joint Centre for Urban Design at Oxford Polytechnic (later to become Oxford Brookes University). My contribution ENVIRONMENTAL IMPROVEMENT: A FAIRY TALE OF OUR TIMES examined Rod Hackney's groundbreaking work at Black Road Macclesfield – a town that was to become an important part of my life.

BEYOND BOLLARDS was a facetious contribution to

RIBAJs "35 under 35" self-promotion issue in 1977. It was the first and mercifully last poem I have ever published, inspired by the peerless William Topaz McGonagall.

Some great places have benefited from the absence of regeneration and the mediocrity of corporate retail investment. PRODUCING THE GOODS for *Green Places* (2006) was a hymn of praise for Bury's tremendous market and a tirade about crap/clone towns.

I've always been ambivalent about mainstream "heritage" thinking, conservatism with a small "c". DOMESDAY for *Place North West* was a response to the English Heritage 2008 "Heritage at Risk Register".

WINNING – also for *Place North West* in 2008 – is a quiz taking the piss out of the development/design/ regeneration professionals.

EVERYTHING YOU WANTED TO KNOW ABOUT REGENERATION (2007)

But were afraid to ask

What is regeneration?
As everyone knows, it's the title of a 1977 Roy Orbison album. It's whitewashing the back yard. And it's about transforming areas with economic, social and environmental problems.

Where is this regeneration?
There's urban regeneration in city centres and the deprived "doughnut" areas around them. There's rural regeneration: every sheep in Cumbria now has broadband, a website and many are active bloggers. Now, the regeneration glitterati are talking about "suburban regeneration".

Is my area being regenerated?
If you stumble back from the pub to find that your Victorian terraced house has been flattened, the answer is yes. You were living in a Housing Market Renewal Area. Other warning signs are invitations to "consultation" meetings in draughty community centres.

Why so many Rs?
This is a mystery. In the 50s there was post-war "Reconstruction"; the 60's brought "Revitalisation"; the 70s "Renewal"; the 80's "Redevelopment" (with a blip of "Renaissance"); the 90s "Regeneration". In the naughties we finally moved on to the next letter of the alphabet – S. S stands for "Sustainability".

Is my community sustainable?
A good question. If your street is gridlocked with gas-

guzzling, toddler-crushing SUVs driven by mums heading for Sainsburys to buy imported Peruvian asparagus that has clocked up staggering air miles, probably not.

Who are the regenerators?
15,000 people in the Northwest – according to one survey – claim to be working in regeneration. The architects are the ones dressed in black. The council officers wear shiny M & S suits. The ones with beards and backpacks are in the voluntary sector. Some of them spend their time applying for money – this is called bidding. Others check whether the money is being spent. Others go to meetings. A few actually do things: this is called delivery.

Why so many regeneration initiatives?
If there were no new initiatives, what would the Whitehall Sir Humphreys do? What would government ministers launch? All governments must have new regeneration initiatives. All councillors must have partnership boards to attend.

What's the vision?
WAGs have observed that the Northwest has more visions than Mother Theresa and more pilots than Ryanair, Easyjet and the RAF combined. Nothing can be done without pilot projects, visions, missions, strategies, action and delivery plans, and targets.

Why are there so many logos on everything?
Wise regenerators know that the best way to silence the opposition is to make them your partner.

Isn't this just throwing good public money after bad?
Yes…and no. There are areas in our at region that have been subjected to serial regeneration since the sixties and still

suffer poor housing and environments, high crime and far too many unemployed and demoralised people. But there are also places that have been transformed.

Such as?
Vauxhall in Liverpool, New East Manchester, and Salford Quays, to name but three.

Is there a risk of reinventing the wheel?
Yes. The same terrible mistakes are made again and again. Regeneration really is difficult.

Any heroes?
There certainly are. There are exceptional developers and local authority people and architects and other professionals. And, in surprising places, there are community leaders, "real people" who've fought for and led the transformation of their areas.

And the next big thing in regeneration?
Well, it was the S word – sustainability. There's no future in business as usual. The low-carbon economy is not a cut price version of the Atkins Diet. Climate change is the big one. We thought. Now it's "placemaking". But, doesn't P come before R and S? We're rewinding! Pass the smelling salts, Sir Humphrey…

ENVIRONMENTAL IMPROVEMENT (1978):

A fairy tale of our times

Improving the environment of older housing areas is a major urban renewal challenge. There are possibilities for the urban designer to contribute as a facilitator of socially responsive processes.

Once upon a time, back in the mysterious and dark Middle Ages, there was a sleepy little market town. It was on the edge of a plain and overlooked by beautiful, rolling green hills. It was a pleasant setting for the unspectacular lives and deaths of the townspeople. The seasons came and went and change was very slow. Then, quite rapidly, the town began to grow very fast. This was the beginning of what historians were later to call the Industrial Revolution. Factories and workshops sprung up, in which machines were used to make fine garments from silk. Then came the railway and a magnificent new canal leading to nearby cities and far beyond. And for the increasing numbers of townspeople, hundreds of new houses were built. Most of these were in neat brick terraces arranged in rectangular blocks.

Now, one particular block of houses was built by the owner of a local brick factory for his workers. It was at the very edge of the town, by the canal, and with fine views from its high position. The families who lived there were happy with their new homes. Generations passed and the houses, like most of the others in the neighbourhood, began to need expensive repairs and improvements. Still, the families who lived in them were reasonably content, even though they didn't have such modern conveniences as bathrooms or inside lavatories. By this time, the houses belonged to several small landlords who simply couldn't afford the cost of expensive renovation.

One day, an official from the Town Council came to look at the houses. He decided that the houses were unfit: they were to be cleared away and the residents would have to find somewhere else to live or rent more modern houses or flats provided by the Council. Well, none of the residents wanted to move. But most of them believed that the Council would be very slow in doing anything definite and that moving would be very far in the future. Life went on very much as before.

Then a young architect bought one of the houses and came to live in the block. He asked the Council to help him to modernise his house with an improvement grant – money towards the cost of building work. As the houses were to be cleared away, the Council refused. The architect felt very annoyed about this and, with his neighbours, formed a Residents Action Group. They marched on the Town Hall, wrote to the local newspapers, contacted the town councillors and campaigned in every way they could think of for the houses to be saved. What they wanted was for the block to be designated as a General Improvement Area (GIA). This would mean that with Council and Government money – as well as their own – the houses and their surroundings could be renewed. They drew up plans and estimated costs, carefully proving that this was possible. Eventually, the Council agreed.

The young architect drew up more detailed plans. The residents arranged to buy their houses from their landlords. Loans and grants and all kinds of complicated agreements were organised. Building contractors began the improvement work and the residents themselves spent a great deal of time helping with it to reduce the costs. After tremendous efforts, and all sorts of difficulties, the improvements were completed. All of the houses were transformed, just as the individual families wanted and were able to afford. The spaces between them looked better than anybody had imagined possible, with paths and walls and trees and plants and even a few parking spaces. Everyone was proud of the improvements and delighted to be able to stay in their houses. The Mayor said: *"God helps those that help themselves"*. And they are all living happily ever after.

So, "What's so special about that fairy tale" you might ask, "a happy ending but but so what?" Well, a lot of people believed that it was special. Journalists wrote about what the residents had done, television crews came to film them, the young architect became famous and successful, and a leading spokesman for "community architecture" and the Government gave the scheme an award. The place was Macclesfield, near Manchester. The block was in Black Road and the architect was Rod Hackney. The residents' campaign began in 1973, and the improvements have now been completed for more than three years.

The proverbial visiting spaceman or, for that matter, almost any Third World squatter, would find it astonishing that events in Black Road are widely seen to be remarkable and have generated such an enormous volume of media attention. Basically, a small group of residents – with expert help and local authority support – successfully devoted some of their time and energy to a co-operative effort to improve their individual houses and communal external environment.

Black Road has been acclaimed as the first example of area improvement in Britain initiated, managed and largely self-built by the residents themselves. The public sector has benefited: expenditure on improvement grants was about two-thirds less than the cost of the alternative: slum clearance and the provision of thirty-three new houses. The semi-public spaces in the scheme are the management and maintenance responsibility of the residents and this represents a continuous cost saving. The residents have benefited: their future is secure and the block has been included, ironically, in a Conservation Area.

The basic ingredients of the success of the process were: a stable and cohesive group of residents able to co-operate together in their own interests; the almost continuous on-site presence of Hackney as a facilitator; and an exceptionally flexible and supportive local authority capable of imaginatively negotiating the financial and organisational constraints on self-help. The implications of Black Road for the practice of architecture have been widely discussed. As Hook (1) has pointed out: *"Up to now we have seen only too clearly the dangers of the (architectural) profession subscribing unconditionally to centrally determined housing programmes that aim at rapid political returns by limiting alternatives and speculating in consumer preferences. Happenings at Black Road, Macclesfield may convince architects that, rather than dictating through authority, they should develop supplementary modes of professional service that can influence through a more soundly based understanding."*

Purely in terms of scale, renewing a single block of housing and its immediate environment could be seen as an architectural problem. But there are implications of the process and the relationship between the various parties involved for the wider, urban design level operation of renewing vast tracts of decaying inner urban housing areas. These implications must be seen in the context of the current state of evolution of housing and environmental renewal policies and methods.

By international standards, Britain has a relatively long history of public sector intervention in housing. Before the Second World War, this was largely focused on setting standards for private development and on the construction of new public sector housing for rent. Since the War, the strategy of improvement of privately-owned housing, with the aid of public sector grants, has gradually shifted into a central position. There have been several stages in the evolution of improvement policies. In 1949, improvement grants were first made available to eligible landlords and owner-occupiers. But during the early sixties, it became clear that there was an operational logic to concentrating resources in selected areas. It also became clear that improvement to the public, external environment of these areas could be a necessary aspect of improving housing quality. Various pilot projects were mounted and a series of problems identified, including the organisational difficulties of local authority interdisciplinary efforts, particularly in environmental improvement implementation, and the complexity of identifying residents' attitudes to, and priorities for, environmental works.

Finally, the 1969 Housing Act introduced the tool of GIAs. Within these, which were to be designated by local authorities, higher rates of improvement grants to owners and landlords were to be made available than elsewhere. Co-ordinated programmes of environmental improvement were to be carried out by local authorities as an incentive to individual, voluntary house improvement (2). Public participation was to be an integral part of the process of environmental improvement.

A number of legislative changes have occurred since the 1969 Housing Act, partly in response to its failure in quantitative terms. And local authorities must operate within patterns of legislation determined by central government. In Britain there are now relatively few slums for which clearance and redevelopment is the only solution. But there are still enormous quantities of older urban housing physically capable of improvement. Much of this housing stands in environments physically capable of renewal and adaptation towards meeting current and future expectations for – for example – pedestrian safety, parking provision and open space. In all, about one third of Britain's total housing stock dates from before 1919. A very high proportion of this is in private ownership. Increasingly, more recent interwar, and even post-war housing – particularly in the public sector – is becoming unacceptable to existing – and potential- tenants. A vivid example of this is a 900-unit Council scheme in Hulme, Manchester, completed in 1970; residents have been campaigning for its demolition and replacement with "real homes".

The interlocking processes of housing and environmental deterioration, and increasing popular housing and environmental aspirations, underline the obvious fact that housing and environmental improvement is, and will remain, a major political and economic challenge. The basic solution to the problem of housing renewal is in adequate financial incentives to individual improvement. While the individual house may be privately controlled, the external environment as experienced by users of an area is formed and controlled by a myriad of forces. In terms of the perception of its users it is public property. The solution to the problem of environmental renewal in response to community priorities is far from clear.

In some ways, the nature of this challenge is underlined by events in Black Road. The initial difficulties were in obtaining access to the resources of the public sector. Environmental improvement to the communal spaces was essentially a question of management rather than of design – negotiating agreement between all of the residents about what should be done. But its real significance is that the residents worked together and contributed their own labour saving a great deal of money in physically implementing the environmental works. But Black Road is a tiny area with a relatively homogenous population. If the process of improvement that took place there can be described as community architecture, the process of area environmental improvement in its application to entire areas, as opposed to isolated, single blocks of houses, should be described as community urban design. At least its aims can be clearly identified: to raise residents' satisfaction with the environmental quality of what they perceive to be their local area. But how?

Most local authorities have assumed (encouraged by government advice)(3) that increasing residents' satisfaction with their local environment can be achieved through a co-ordinated set of one-off physical improvements (such as traffic control schemes or tree planting), devised and implemented with token participation of the residents affected. Participation is seen as a tool for smoothing the path of the authority's proposals. Occasionally, this approach has succeeded. Frequently, it has not: even in the rare cases where the authority has the organisational capacity to carry out an adequate programme, there tend to be to inherent sets of limitations of such approaches.

Firstly, experts' perceptions of priorities for action may well be markedly different from residents'. And there is already a substantial body of research on environmental satisfaction which suggests that, apart from fairly general agreement about environmental necessities (such as street lighting), residents – even of the same social class – may not share common concerns about the quality of their environment. In particular, their attitudes are likely to be shaped by their stage in the family life cycle. The range of residents' concerns may span social, functional and symbolic aspects of their environment: these may not neatly dovetail with the improvement possibilities embodied within such narrowly-conceived legislative tools as GIAs.

Comprehensive physical improvements may necessitate a range of actions, possibly including one-off improvements such as tree-planting. But of equal or even more importance may be basic maintenance, such as pavement resurfacing, or improved regular services such as street cleaning. Many aspects of raising environmental quality cannot be tackled through physical improvements at all. The only hope of ensuring that the solutions that are possible within economic and legislative constraints are even beginning to be appropriate is to extend the boundaries of decision-making to include those who are affected by the problems. Just as in Black Road, the basis of a responsive approach is in a partnership between the authorities and those they should be serving.

The second disadvantage of current approaches is simply their inability, through lack of financial and manpower resources, to tackle the problem of poor environments on anything like the scale required. Nationally, the effect of GIA legislation in improving environmental quality has been minimal(4). But a vast resource exists in the form of the time and energy of ordinary people – as Black Road and countless other examples of voluntary involvement in self-help demonstrate. However, if people are to contribute their time and energy to improving their environment in a partnership with local authorities – which are the only agencies with the power to manage area-level programmes – two basic conditions must be met. Residents must believe that environmental improvements are necessary. They must be convinced that their positive involvement will speed the improvements that they perceive to be priorities. Again, this points to a decision-making partnership with the local authority.

The nature of such a partnership raises all kinds of questions about the relationship between the residents of an area and the almost incomprehensible machine that is the typical local authority. Just as in Black Road, what is required is a facilitator acting as an intermediary between residents and the authority. The key role of the facilitator is not as an interpreter or adviser on residents' problems (in the conventional professional sense) but as a manager of the processes of environmental change. Even the most elementary types of change, such as closing a road, necessitate complex procedures which, on an area level, simply cannot be handled by residents themselves. There is a fundamental difference between the role of facilitator and the role of advocacy planner.

The media-model of the unified community battling with a unified and faceless bureaucracy can be a reasonable interpretation of events in single-issue conflicts (should the houses be demolished or not?). And Hackney's contribution to community action in the initial stages of saving the houses at Black Road was that of expert advocacy.

However, area environmental improvement is not quite as simple as a single-issue conflict. It is a complex process of change which may expose conflicts within the local authority itself, between the local authority and residents, and even between different groups of residents. It may be a micro-political battleground. While one role for a facilitator may be in resolving conflicts within the local authority, there may also be instances where the resolution of conflict between different groups of residents is simply impossible. However, while resident involvement in shaping environmental improvement programmes and even in implementing them can result in stalemate, direct experience of conflict may be a form of community development. At the very least, it will be a form of community development more vivid than the passive consumption of evangelistic bureaucracy.

The urban designer, whether employed directly by a local authority, or indirectly as a private consultant, and faced with a problem such as contributing to the environmental quality of a housing area, is inevitably shackled by institutional and operational constraints. Only through creating a role as a facilitator or, at the very least, perceiving his role as that of facilitator, can he hope to push these constraints to their limits just as Hackney has attempted to do in an architectural context.

The direction in which he will push will be determined by

his conception of accountability. Within our present hierarchical and unresponsive system of environmental control, he is very unlikely to find himself neatly slotted into a position in which he is directly responsible to his real clients: the users of the areas with which he is concerned. But there are possibilities for carving out a role as a kind of institutional subversive. Firstly, urban design is not a profession with a clear arena of operation. Secondly, the nature of most local authorities is so fragmented that the crosser of professional and departmental boundaries – essential in the management of environmental improvement programmes – may be able to manipulate the system in an unusually productive way.

In the hazy middle ground between despair in the face of institutional unresponsiveness and optimism in the face of ordinary people's capacity to involve themselves in improving their environment, there are possibilities. At the interface of institutional inaction and community action there are opportunities for the urban designer as facilitator to contribute to the very serious problem of environmental poverty in housing areas. How long will it be before we can write not just one fairy story, but a bookshelf of volumes in which the heroes are the residents of housing areas and the good fairies are urban designers?

BEYOND BOLLARDS (1977)

Beautiful city with yer troubled inner bits
You're an awful sight!
And I'm most disturbed by yer plight.
Majestic Architecture! It doesnae seem to me
That practising You
Helps me or the problems a single bawbee
So what I'm into is Urban Design
And interpreting the environment to yours, his and mine
It started with stories for papers like Building Design
And working on a GIA where the residents were fine
Researching the mysteries of Urban Design
Working on kids' books for a time
Because we need to find a way
Of giving Maw, Paw and Oor Wullie
A very much bigger say!

(Apologies to William McGonagall, Poet and Tragedian).

Nominated by the editors *RIBA Journal*

PRODUCING THE GOODS (2006)

Pigs' feet, honeycomb, cow heel pieces and black tripe at only £3.80/kg! A slice of Chadwick's legendary black pudding in a barm with a dollop of Barton's piccalilli sauce! A nightmare vision of veggie hell? No, it's Bury Market. And it's official: Bury is the best market in Britain, proud winner of the Market of the Year competition, the cream of 1700 markets across the country.

Granny Singletons tasty Lancs cheese, glistening wild trout, bunches of fresh asparagus, mint humbugs, clothes *"over-makes from famous brands and slight seconds"*, used DVDs, naff mobile phone covers and all the trashy bric-a-brac of modern life. A bucket of pigs' ears as pet treats beside a hallucinatory display of dog leads of every colour of the rainbow – truly a cornucopia of wonders! And as if the colours, smells, tastes and people were not enough, the cheery, brassy tooting of Hebden Bridge Junior Band as the icing on the cake.

With 500 years of experience, 200,000 square feet of shopping over 370 stalls and 250,000 visitors a week, Bury is the largest market in the Northwest of England. Its centrepiece is a state-of-the-art (nineteen-sixties actually) steel, glass and concrete fish and meat hall with a range *"from prawns to shark"*. All within two minutes of Bury Metrolink stop.

At the other end of the spectrum and two minutes from London Bridge station, Borough Market in London: shining with glorious fruit and veg and feasts of organic, gourmet and exotic produce. Its cafes and restaurants have spread to the surrounding streets: a foodie's paradise as well as a vibrant, joyful townscape.

No sign in Bury or London then of the nationwide decline of the markets industry. Or the municipal neglect or misguided planning that sweeps away the messiness of the market in favour of the neatness of bland redevelopment. Markets were the reason for many towns to exist. Markets are our oldest and most successful form of exchange. In its recently published *"Manifesto for Markets"*, campaigning group Common Ground argues for local distinctiveness, reducing food miles and providing outlets for small producers. We are reminded that market halls can be fine and successful buildings in function and design and that *"the shapes, buildings and ghosts of a market and its artefacts...are important cultural memories"*. Markets are dynamic, reflecting the comings and goings of new communities and the things they buy.

Elsewhere, *"Crap Towns"* is a bestseller. Grumpy people vote for the crapness of their town. The blogosphere is fizzing with anti-corporate-retail ranting. The Tescopoly website: *"This is not Tesco...every little hurts...so get your groceries somewhere else...support local business"*. The documentary film *"Wal-Mart: The High Cost of Low Price"* has been on general release. Tesco and Wal-Mart domination, where will it end? Tesco hospitals? Wal-Mart water?

We have all experienced the alienation of the shopping mall, disinfected and protected from the possibility of having to look a *Big Issue* vendor in the eye. We have suffered pangs of despair in the edge of town car park ringed by MFI and Pet World crinkly sheds. The Burger King wrappers flutter in the wind. Is this it? Is this the epicentre of our civilisation, we ask? Anytown? Anywhere?

The greatest urbanist of the twentieth century, Jane Jacobs, died in April at the age of 88 after a lifetime of provocation. She wrote and campaigned tirelessly against mediocrity, crapness, neatness and "zoning" and for diversity, colour, messiness and street life. She would have appreciated the buzz of Bury Market. She would have enjoyed the cosmopolitan diversity of Borough Market. Her spirit lives on in the *"Clone Towns"* survey by UK think tank The New

Economics Foundation. Of the towns surveyed, a shocking 42 per cent were classified as clone towns – *"places where the individuality of high street shops has been replaced by a monochrome strip of global and national chains, somewhere that could easily be mistaken for dozens of bland town centres across the country"*.

NEF attacks the "triple whammy" of clone stores. They bleed the local economy of money. They contribute nothing to the social glue that holds communities together. They steal the identity of towns and cities. The argument that the inexorable rise of the big retailers is all about choice is nonsense: in the end, there will be no choice at all. More than 20,000 high street shops have gone to the wall since 1997 and the trend continues.

Is there no alternative? Well, yes. Town planning and public sector investment in "regeneration" must be smarter. The Competition Commission needs to get a grip on anti-competitive practices through its investigation of the big supermarkets. And we consumers can vote with our feet and head for the market. So, here's to colour, diversity, recycled shopping bags, a zipped-up wallet and the next Metrolink to Bury.

"Producing the Goods 2 – Markets and Market Places" is published by Common Ground.

THE PUNCTUATION MARKS OF HISTORY (2008)

"...the punctuation marks of history"
                                              Winston Churchill

What was he on about?
Battlefields.

What's the connection between battlefields, shipwrecks, monuments, and parks and gardens?
They're all on the twenty-first century Domesday Book *"Heritage at Risk"* which itemises threatened assets. The 2008 edition has just been published by English Heritage.

But there are no threatened battlefields or shipwrecks in this great Northwest region of ours?
Surprisingly, that is true. But there are 135 listed buildings and scheduled monuments. Many of these have been registered since the 1999 baseline. Some present intractable difficulties.

It's all redundant churches then?
Far from it. There is a group of three World War One aircraft hangers at Ellesmere Port. Warrington Bank Quay's dramatic transporter bridge is rusting. Lowther Castle near Penrith, a gothic country house, closed in 1935; the contents were stripped out in 1947 and the roof removed in 1957. Fort Perch Rock in new Brighton is a fortified lighthouse built in 1826. The Tate and Lyle Sugar Silo in Regent Road Liverpool dates from 1955-57. And all travellers of Piccadilly Station in Manchester will know the sad spectacle of the Police and Fire Station in London Road built in 1901.

Who cares?
We do. We love costume drama, snobbery with violence, Laura Ashley frocks and heritage. A survey by Stockport Council at last year's Heritage Open Days found that 72 per cent of visitors *"experienced increased pride in the Borough"* as a result of attending a Heritage Open Day event.

WINNING – IN 2008 (2007)

With 2007 almost forgotten, it's time to speculate wildly about 2008: Faster! Smarter! Bigger! Better! Time to take stock. How are we doing? Are we tuned into the zeitgeist? How do we win?

My first *Cut Out 'n Keep Interactive Personal Assessment Solutions Questionnaire TM* provides you with the answer. Calm down, clear your head, and answer the questions. No conferring, no phoning a friend or shouting across the office. No Google searching. You need to know the truth! One point for each correct answer.

Q1. Hobnob is:
(a) the leading social networking website for top professionals
(b) the classic biscuit
(c) a powerful contacts management system

Q2. Key dress code / fashion statement for alpha males for spring '08:
(a) tie
(b) no tie
(c) string vest peeking out from open-necked shirt

Q3. The first pioneering site for eco-homes in the Northwest is:
(a) Wilmslow
(b) Bickershaw Colliery
(c) Skelmersdale

Q4. The politically correct jargon for what used to be called urban design is:
(a) place making
(b) place shaping
(c) PlacesMatter!

Q5. Spot the odd one out:
(a) Lancashire – red rose county
(b) Manchester – original modern?
(c) Cumbria – Britain's nuclear county

Q6. MIPIM is the acronym for:
(a) The World's Premier Real Estate Summit
(b) Massive Piss-up in the Med
(c) Member of the Institute of Personal Investment Marketeers

Q7. Who said "Back to black"?:
(a) Amy Winehouse
(b) Habitat
(c) John Prescott

Q8. The fastest growing phenomenon amongst business leaders in 2007 was:
(a) dogging
(b) snogging
(c) blogging

Q9. Banksy is:
(a) a Bruntwood building in Liverpool
(b) the internationally renowned graffiti artist
(c) a tributary of the River Mersey

Q10. How many RICS members are there in the North of England?:
(a) 10,000
(b) 15,000
(c) 25,000

Q11. MAMBO is:
(a) miles and miles of bugger all – a Whitehall civil servant's informed assessment of this great region of ours
(b) a specialised form of Brazilian hiphop
(c) a feature-rich content management system

6 BANNED WORDS AND BULLSHIT BINGO

Every picture tells a story – as Rod Stewart pointed out. That's certainly not true of every word, sentence or paragraph. Readers of *Private Eye's* "Pseud's Corner" – in which I once had the privilege of being quoted – know this very well. Language is so easy to misuse, abuse. I've always been intensely irritated by the "economic development" charlatans (world class cross cutting themes, anyone?) and business drivellers (going forward).

The Northwest Regional Project unleashed a nightmare plethora of visions, missions and strategy waffle egged on by European Commission Structural Funds babble. Remarkably, this is alive and well today. Orwell continues to turn in his grave.

ARCHISPEAK for *Architectural Design* in 1974 attacked visual obfuscation by architects. I was job architect for a commercial practice in London that was brilliantly successful in manipulating dire megaprojects through the planning system. I learned the power of presentation – strategically placed Letraset, lush hanging planting cascading from the decks, and elegant stickpeople loving the malls.

BANNED! for *Place North West* tackled public sector jargon. I was thrilled with the Local Government Association's 2008 list of 100 "non words".

Parallel nonsense has been emerging throughout my lifetime in "place branding" – Who now remembers – *"Liverpool – city of change and challenge"* or *"Manchester – up and going"*? – up itself and going down the pan, as critics quipped at the time. WHAT'S IN A NAME? also for *Place North West* (2008) has a go.

ARCHISPEAK (1974)

Prostituting visual language is a game traditionally played by a wide spectrum of the design professions. Hanging gardens of Babylon planting, cup-final crowd open spaces and orgasmic skies are part of the graphic mythology that promotes visions of an existence somewhere between precast concrete and Utopia.

The gang-banging of words, however, is not a tongue-in-cheek activity in these professions in which the creation of visual images is the central concern and language only a secondary tool:

Language facilitates communication within the group, it also crystallises cultural differences, and actually heightens the barriers between groups" (1)

To be more specific, the collective unconscious of the architectural profession has formed an interlocking set of literary barriers, or word games, similar in their deceptive nature to the more familiar visual cliches. Here are a few examples:

The Mrs Malaprop-in-Granny-Glasses Tendency
The objective of this type of word game is to convince the outsider that architects are custodians of a definitive and impenetrable way of seeing. The game is a guilty response to the intellectual untidiness of design and the difficulty of reconciling the dilettante and cool analytical approaches. Example:

"Colin Rowe prefers an urban cycle that he calls 'collage', which at first sight might suggest something analogous, but is, rather, part of an alien procedure that prefers a consistency within the replaced elements..." (2)

The Leonardo Tendency
Plagiarising words and concepts from several disciplines is

a subtle technique intended to give the impression of breadth of thinking: the wider view. This game is often played when there is nothing to be said. Example:

"*But our search for adaptive systems should have a prime objective, to produce an environment to which the ordinary individual at any level of intensity can reconcile himself without the intolerable effort and stress of his own mental and physical adaptation*" (3)

The Siena Tendency

The game is never played in Italy. Optimistic use of Italian features conjures up travel-brochure visions of sun-drenched piazzas and organic townscapes. Alternatively, blank verse or even the stream-of-consciousness method is employed to elevate the banal to the spiritual. Example:

"*We wanted the elemental qualities of monastic cells. A place with the traditional qualities of withdrawal. Roof to floor slit light. I like the glazing looking down. I dare say some people get vertigo, but...*" (4)

The Nostradamus Tendency

Propaganda as a substitute for reasoned argument, prophesy, sloganising and the offering of instant solutions are the main features of this game. Action is advocated in a medium unrelated to the nature of the problem. Example:

"*Society is filled with a violent desire for something which it may obtain or may not. Everything lies in that; everything depends on the effort made and the attention paid to these alarming symptoms. Architecture or revolution. Revolution can be avoided*"(5)

The 1984 Tendency

You too can have a go at this game. Using these tendencies as a rough guide, leaf through any back-number of *AD*, and see how many doublethink phrases, sentences and even entire articles you can collect. After a few tries you'll want to develop your own tendencies. It's so much fun you'll find it difficult to stop. George Orwell reckoned that the age of doublespeak will fully come into its own by 1984. That gives us just ten years to go!

BANNED! (2008)

Multi-disciplinary place-shaping of sustainable communities:
BANNED!

Cross-cutting stakeholder partnership, signposting quick wins:
BANNED!

Multi-agency dialogue engaging users in resource allocation:
BANNED!

Predictors of beaconicity*:
BANNED!

Banned?
Yes. All of these words. Honestly. The Local Government Association has compiled a list of 100 "non-words". It has been sent to all local councils and public sector bodies. Sir Simon Miller of the LGA: *"Without explaining what a council does in proper English, then local people will fail to understand its relevance to them or why they should bother to turn out and vote. Unless information is given to people to explain why their council matters, then local democracy will be threatened with extinction... why do we have to have coterminous stakeholder engagement when we could just talk to people instead?"*

And why do they say: "slippage in resource allocation" when what they really mean is "err...cheque's not in the post" and "scaling back empowerment" when they mean "get stuffed" and "transformational coterminous shared priorities" when it's obvious they'd be in the same pub on a Friday?

Fine, but has this gone too far?
What's wrong with:
world-class; estate agent; luxury; offshore; MIPIM; spread-

betting; financial instruments; superquango; AGMA; portfolio; rebranding; congestion charging; Ken Livingston? Nothing; they're not on the list…yet! But could this be the start of Stasi-like, top-down (whoops, sorry, "top-down" is banned) directives…infringement of human rights…attack on freedom of speech…end of civilisation as we know it?

And professionals need jargon!
It's one thing for local authorities to ban jargon and use plain English. They don't have to earn their living. But how can professional fees be earned without jargon?

Where would our legal friend Hugefee and his mates be if they couldn't keep the clock running as they bait each other with legal obscurities? Magnatum scandalum, to put it mildly. And our architect friend Bowtie and his ramblings about spatial integrity? Tweedie the planning consultant droning on about PPGs? Isambard the engineer enthusing about bending moments? Abfab the PR raving on about pre-consultation horizontal pitches? This could be the thin end of a very dangerous wedge.

So no good will come of it?
There's another side of the coin. We're all confused. We're drowning in jargon, sinking in crap. Sussed out Futurebuilders? Aligned? Double devolution? NEET? No? Well, they're just a few of the treats in the *"Glossary of Regeneration and Local Economic Development"*, all fifty pages of it, published by Manchester-based think tank CLES.

Where can I get help?
Self-help is the only answer. One sheet of paper, twenty-five words and a pencil is all it takes to play Bullshit Bingo. Draw a grid and enter the jargon words of your choice. Tick them off as they surface at the meeting. As bullshitbingo.co.uk explains: *"Create meetings where participants strive to present*

complex ideas in simple no-nonsense language, determined to win with a clear home run in the Bullshit Bingo stakes". And, what's more, there are no training manuals! No consultants! No Bullshit Bingo inspirational workshops!

Or?

Meeting time again. Lights dimmed. Powerpoint hell, blizzards of bullshit. As ever, colleagues drift off into daydream la-la land. The more driven are power napping. But you are alert, focused, ears tuned to perfection, pencil poised over the bullshit bingo grid. The magic moment arrives: "BINGO!" you scream triumphantly. Carafes of water splashed all over the papers! Startled looks! Rabbits in headlights!

*Predictors of beaconicity? Something to do with pregnancy tests, maybe? Belisha beacons? Cities? Wrong ! – it means: *"which local authorities are most likely to apply to, or be short listed and awarded through the Beacon scheme".* You couldn't make it up.

WHAT'S IN A NAME? (2008)

No!
- cloth-capped pensioner, ferret on shoulder, gripping KwikSave bag stuffed with betting slips:
 "*Effing disgrace, it were bad enough t'council scrapping t'pies at pensioners' xmas dinner and forcefeedin' us effin' fair trade fruit...but this is going too far...NO!*"

Maybe
- our friend hoo_d_ie_crack_ texts from the blogosphere:
 "*OMG!...IMHO...colours...yeah...whirlie...dunno...no... MAYBE*"

Yes
- man in suit from the council Economic Development Department (the ones with the rubber plant along the corridor from the Chief Exec):
 "*Knowledge economy... inward investment... global positioning...subregional...competitiveness...sectors...blah...YES*"

Yes
- man with red glasses and the aluminium manbag:
 "*Brand values...black is the new white...creative quarter... ...Helvetica medium...YES*"

That's enough vox pops. What are they on about?
Place branding, of course. Doesn't matter whether it's a mall (*Liverpool One*), a town (*One Oldham*), a city (*Manchester – original modern*), a county (*Cumbria – Britain's nuclear county**) or a nation (*Cool Britannia*). Everybody has an opinion on names, logos, colours and straplines. Guaranteed to electrify even the doziest. Acres of vox pops in local papers. Pages of deranged letters to the editor in green ink. Mayhem in the blogosphere. Craziness in the phone-ins.

Surely this is all marketing froth and we should be investing in something useful like the Olympics or more bobbies on the beat?
No. Place branding has proved itself through the ages. The Romans did a good job with their empire: even the donkeys, the white vans of antiquity, knew that they were Romans. One of the pioneers of branding, Lord Leverhulme of Pears Soap and countless other branded products fame, didn't miss a trick with *Port Sunlight*.

And places are competing, are they not?
Yes. Famously, Glasgow decided that it was miles better (than Edinburgh – and everywhere else). Now it's moved on to: *Glasgow – Scotland with Style* (cheerily headbutting Edinburgh…no style…feral bag ladies roaming the streets, fur coats, nae knickers and moths fluttering out of their wild hair).

But you can't just make up names?
You can…Cannibal (or Cantril as strangers sometimes referred to it) Farm in Knowsley was rebranded *Stockbridge Village*. Manchester's uber hip *Northern Quarter* is a complete fabrication…and the name has stuck. Only time will tell, but people are starting to speak of *Spinningfields*.

A dangerous game, surely?
Certainly is. Like public art, place branding can be a triumph (*I love New York*) or go horribly wrong. Early New Labour's *Cool Britannia* – Gerry Halliwell in her Union Jack frock and Liam swigging champers at Number 10 – turned sour. It's already a historical footnote. *Cool Britannia* will be remembered only by the 1967 Bonzo Dog Doo-Dah Band song of that name.

Remember Manchester's *"We're up and going"*?
Exactly. This 1997 nonsense (Up what – ourselves? Going where – Strangeways? KwikSave? Hell?) enraged the Manc creatives. They formed the McEnroe Group, tagline *"you cannot be serious"* and successfully drove a stake through its heart.

Better be careful, then?
Careful is not the same as boring and lacking in ambition. Think of France: Burgundy, or Germany: Bavaria, or Italy: Tuscany. Their regions have wonderful names you can feel and smell and lick. And here: who wants to lick the East Midlands or England's Northwest? north-west is a direction, not a place. It's like living in a motorway sign.

So it's two steps forward and one step back?
Yes. The luckless inhabitants of Vale Royal – quite a classy 1974 invention – are about to find themselves living in a road sign – West Cheshire – when their Council is abolished. On the other hand, it's goodbye to East Lancashire (where?) and hello to Pennine Lancashire or *"PL your new favourite place"*.

What does the future hold?
The places will tell you themselves: get ready for the talking bollards and the singing bus shelters and chatty parking meters. There will be no escape. You might not know where you are. But they will.

* *All right – I made that one up.*

7 ART WILL SAVE THE WORLD

Well, possibly not on its own, but art certainly makes places less dreary. Architecture – frozen music – is of course the greatest of the arts. I haven't written much about architecture and architects since my *Building Design* journalism period in the seventies. And, as a graduate of the modernist tradition of the Edinburgh College of Art School of Architecture, I've never escaped the modernist/Bauhaus ideology beaten into us. It was a joy working in Sunley (now City) Tower – part of a fine brutalist megastructure in the heart of Manchester.

But public art – "high" and commissioned; "inadvertant" and discovered; "subversive" and sprayed – is a gift to the flaneur and amateur street photographer (like me).

The Northwest Regional Project enabled courageous investment in public art, ignoring the philistine whingeing of squelchers. The Northwest Development Agency – funder in chief – was mercifully free of democracy and nervous councillors.

BUT IS IT ART? for *Place North West* in 2007 in praise of public art is a reminder of Braque's case that art is meant to disturb.

EYES WIDE SHUT: A GOLDEN AGE OF PUBLIC ART for *Green Places* in 2006 goes further and I claim that this is the golden age of public art. Alright, comparisons with Renaissance Florence might undermine the argument, but there's a serious point here.

In HOW DO YOU WANT YOUR CITY? for *Green Futures* in 2006 I take a swing at the squelchers and and propose that rather than being perceived as "envirocrime", graffiti can be empowering.

BUT IS IT ART? (2007)

Is that a UFO on Top o' Slate?
Night falls. Blue glow. A huge shining lattice has landed. Rossendale, famous in the international UFO tracking community, is known as "UFO Alley". Rossendale: memorably described by its former council chief executive as the Albania of the Northwest...edgy...mysterious. In fact, *"Halo"* is the fourth and final panopticon. Designed by John Kennedy of Landlab, the 18 metre diameter steel structure is supported on a truncated tripod. Trusses radiating from the conical core support luminous blue rings lit with low energy LEDs. The power comes from a nearby wind farm. A new landmark in Pennine Lancs, or PL, as we must learn to call it.

Why is that traffic warden pink?
She is handing people pink tickets and lollies as she patrols the streets of Keswick, rewarding motorists for their creative parking. The Ministry of Creative Parking (Kate Gilman Brundrett), is one of many artists from around the world, here for Cumbria's FRED Festival (September 28th to October 14th). FRED is claimed to be Europe's largest annual festival of site-specific art. Installations will include Simon Beal's *"Beached"* – 18,000 sandcastles over a 2km stretch near Whitehaven.

Should that man be looking through a hole in the wall?
It's alright. He's peering through one of *"The Peeps: twenty holes in Ancoats"*, revealing surprises from the area's history as a pioneering industrial powerhouse. Long-forgotten tunnels, a bell tower and a lavatory are amongst the treats. Conceived by architect/ artist Dan Dubowitz, visitors must discover *"The Peeps"* for themselves. No signs; no plaques; no logos.

And the camel and sheep on Crosby Beach?
There is no end to the astonishing events triggered by Antony Gormley's magnificent *"Another Place"*. The "iron men" have been a popular, critical and artistic triumph. The campaigners to keep them have finally won the battles and the war. Even the most cutting critics of Prescott's Northern Way have been forced to concede that its financial backing of *"Another Place"* was a masterstroke.

Is that building moving?
Yes; it's the people who are still, stopped in their tracks exiting from Liverpool's Moorfields Station. They are looking up at a great circular slice of the façade of Cross Keys House rotating and twisting. Richard Wilson's *"Turning the Place Over"* has been described as the most daring piece of public art ever commissioned in the UK. Any challengers?

But the Mersey Wave and B of the Bang were a problem?
Teething troubles. Public art fact of life number 1: The squelchers always find something to whinge about. Rome was not built in day. Medieval cathedral builders had endless construction problems and collapses.

Spending taxpayers' money on public so-called "art" is outrageous!
Wrong! Cultural tourism plays a growing part in our economy. It is one of the main reasons for people to visit the UK. And one of the main reasons for visitors from within the UK coming to the Northwest. Crosby Beach has become a destination. Even the most neanderthal economic development types can't fail to notice the swarms of tourists during the Liverpool Biennial, for instance.

It's clever, but is it art?
A really stupid question. Wilfrid Scawen Blunt's view of the

post impressionists (in 1910) helps us here: *"They are not works of art at all, unless throwing a handful of mud against a wall may be called one. They are the works of idleness and impotent stupidity, a pornographic show."* Public art fact of life number 2: there will always be people like Wilfrid. Sod them.

Seriously, though?

More constructively, Braque: *"Art is meant to disturb, science reassure"*. And there's plenty of disturbance to look forward to. Next year, the controversial Turner Prize is coming to Liverpool – its first time out of London. The squelchers are already warming up their vitriol. Public art fact of life number 3: you can't please all of the people all of the time! Celebrate!

EYES WIDE SHUT: A GOLDEN AGE OF PUBLIC ART (2006)

The tiny bird on top of a four-metre bronze pole guarding Liverpool's Anglican Cathedral Oratory is Tracy Emin's *"Roman Standard"*. Commissioned by the BBC, the inevitable question on the BBC website was *"What do you think of public art? Does it enrich the cultural life of the city or is it a waste of money?"*.

Despite the usual chorus of philistines and whingers, it is a thrilling time for "official" public art. 2005 was a bumper year. In London, who could not be moved by Mark Quinn's *"Alison Lapper Pregnant"* on Trafalgar Square's fourth plinth? On the South Bank and then at the Eden Project in Cornwall, the RSA's seven metre *"WEEE Man"* starkly illustrated the three tonnes of electronic waste the average citizen is likely to consume in a lifetime. In Manchester, Thomas Heatherwick's *"B of the Bang"* – the tallest sculpture in the UK and a tribute to the Commonwealth games – was launched with a spectacular firework display. In Newcastle-Gateshead, Spencer Tunick's largest installation to date engaged 1700 nude people on the streets and on the bridges.

At Crosby Beach, Antony Gormley's *"Another Place"* – one hundred life-size bronze figures – pleased the art world and has been adopted by local people. It has been a huge success in transforming a mediocre place into a destination and a setting for extraordinary events. In August, forty of the figures were dressed in white T-shirts and purple capes by Fathers for Justice protesting about the Child Support Agency. Last Christmas, thousands experienced a nativity play in *"Another Place"* with a camel, a donkey, a flock of sheep and, of course, angels.

In Blackpool, hyper-kitsch and art crossed over. For the first time in 126 years, the illuminations stretched beyond the promenade and embraced formal, commissioned "public art" including the worlds biggest glitter ball. It's obvious that public investment in public art carries risks and automatically triggers knee-jerk whingeing. But what a return from the successes! And far better value for money than expensive and wasteful "economic development" littering the landscape with vacant crinkly sheds.

Meanwhile, in the world of "unofficial" public art, there were triumphs as well. Heysham, in the shadow of the nuclear power station, won *"Britain in Bloom 2005"* – wonderful!

But a nadir was the ill-advised appearance by Tony Blair, cleaning graffiti from a wall, and the authoritarian nonsense around the otherwise welcome Clean Neighbourhoods and Environment Act. One person's graffiti, councillor, is another's street art. Street art has a very long history. It can be traced back to the cave paintings at Lascaux. More recent influences are nineteen-seventies Los Angeles hip-hop and global cartoon characters. The elements of street art are tags (the signatures of the artist or the crew), characters, and pieces (derived from masterpieces) – these are full-colour works often focused around a name or word written in funky, stylised fonts. Typical media are paint and markers, stencils, stickers and digital/the web. Street artists have become world-famous, the subject of monographs and exhibitions. The real identity of Banksy – perhaps the most famous exponent of stencilling – is unknown. His "rogue artworks" have ranged from Stone Age shopping trolleys in the British Museum to the iconic anarchist rat climbing over anti-climb paint to the image of a child digging a hole through the Palestine side of the West Bank wall.

The French 123Klan claim that *"You can't stop it – graffiti is bigger than politics and even bigger than the United Nations"*.

Maybe that's a slight overstatement. But the boundaries between the official and the unofficial are becoming blurred. In Newcastle, *"Eye of the Fly"* is an innovative lottery-supported project that uses disused industrial units as blank spaces in which young people experiment in spraying areas. In London, the undercroft of the Hayward Gallery has become unmolested street art/skateboarding territory. Street art is crossing over into marketing of cool stuff. With the exception of sterile, controlled shopping malls, it can be found everywhere.

Attempts to obliterate the possibility of street art by designing out opportunities usually fail. The squelchers – killjoys with their eyes wide shut – will always meet resistance. The best buildings are long-life, loose-fit, low-energy. The best public spaces are loose-fit. Creative people and places need each other.

Banksy sums it up beautifully:

"Imagine a city where graffiti wasn't illegal, a city where everybody could draw whatever they liked, where every street was awash with a million colours and little phrases. Where standing at a bus stop was never boring. A city that feels like a living breathing thing which belongs to everybody not just the estate agents and barons of big business. Imagine a city like that and stop leaning against the wall – it's wet."

HOW DO YOU WANT YOUR CITY? (2006)

How do you want your city? Clean, green, safe... and boring? Alarm bells ring over the government's crackdown on enviro crime. Do funky flyposters and artistic graffiti really degrade the environment? The squelchers and the nanny state need to be challenged.

Dogshit in the park! Graffiti on the walls! Festering mounds of fly-tippings! Hooded feral youths gobbing gum on to beautifully-laid paving stones!

Enviro crime – it disturbs us. It has a daily impact on our lives. And some at least is lucrative crime, too. White van fly-tipper man is in it for the dosh. Fast-moving fly-posting teams defend the territories – sometimes violently – which promoters pay big money to exploit. And the binge drinkers whose bottles, glasses and unspeakable debris carpet town centres at weekends are not the "socially excluded": a heavy night on the town is expensive.

So, on the surface, we should be giving a round of applause for the Clean Neighbourhoods and Environment Act, designed to get to grips with it all. White vans suspected of involvement in fly-tipping can be stopped and searched. Gum-gobbers can be slapped with hefty fines.

So far, so good. But...on-the-spot fines of £75 and upwards for graffiti artists? Is there some confusion here? Could we be starting to lose the plot?

Remember the *"Clone Towns"* report? This brilliant exercise by the New Economics Foundation judged that *"The glass, steel and concrete blandness of identikit chain stores"* had already turned 41per cent of the towns it surveyed into clones, with *"high streets virtually indistinguishable from each other"*. As the report says, *"Many town centres that have undergone substantial regeneration have lost their sense of place and distinctive features"*.

In the US, where the problem is far more advanced than

in Britain, one town has responded with the courageous slogan: *"Keep Louisville Weird"*.

More than 30 years ago, Jane Jacobs's inspiring book *The Death and Life of Great American Cities* urged urban professionals to celebrate the colourful street life that gives neighbourhoods such vitality and character. Fast forward to the National Competitiveness Summit in Manchester last October, where her disciple, Richard Florida (author of *The Rise of the Creative Classes*), unveiled research carried out in cities across the world which concluded that the two things people valued most were their "aesthetic nature" (meaning both their physical environment and their culture), and their diversity.

Conventional measures of the economic performance of cities are completely wrong, Florida argues. What we have to measure instead is human happiness. Few sustainable development aficionados would argue. But he goes further. The evidence is overwhelming, he claims, that *"The places that are most open will win"*. This means that organic, messy, street-level artistic and music scenes have a vital role. *"We must limit the effectiveness of the squelchers – the people who say 'No!',"* says Florida. *"They are afraid of human expression and creativity."*

In which case, what about that Clean Neighbourhoods law? Is it right to make fly-posting a crime in just the same way as mindless vandalism? Is the environment being degraded by the colourful and funky posters brightening the blacked-out windows of an abandoned public building near my office? Is political comment sprayed on plywood building site hoardings damaging anything or anyone?

And then there is street art or, to be politically correct, graffiti. Famously, the eruption of Vesuvius preserved graffiti carved on the walls of Pompeii. Then, as now, there were insults, magic, political comment – words and images. Graffiti can be ambitious in scale and breathtakingly daring in execution. Or it can be modest, almost imperceptible, like the elegant little sticker obliterating the council logo on the bus shelter at the end of my street. It can be artistically thrilling or vacuous – just like any other art form, in fact. And so-called "tagging" – territorial gangs marking public property – is now being overtaken by non-gang-related graffiti art. Artists sign their tags. This is art for art's sake.

Of course some contemporary graffiti is disturbing. Spraying racist abuse hardly adds value to the urban experience. Tagging can be threatening in communities where gang-driven gun and drug crime is endemic.

But…a cardinal principle of sustainable development is that of engagement, empowerment, and participation. Creativity is a dimension of this. Not everybody will be fulfilled by yoghurt-weaving at worthy evening classes. Creative people want to be in lively, diverse, edgy places. The cloners, the squelchers and the nanny state need to be challenged. This even makes economic sense. As Jane Jacobs has said: *"When a place gets boring even the rich leave."*

8 ORIGINAL MODERN...AND RAINING: MANCHESTER

Manchester – the world's first industrial city – was beginning to reverse its long post-industrial decline by the time I began to get to know it in the eighties. The city's confidence, swagger and boosterism continues to accelerate. Due to the rain, the miserabilist tendencies of the Manchester spirit have never disappeared. Happily, they are overwhelmed by ambition, energy and strong leadership. *"If only we could combine Manchester's discipline with Liverpool's passion, just think where we could be"* – a facetious but perceptive quip.

Parts of Greater Manchester suffer from dreadful poverty and shockingly poor life expectancy. A sustainable future for some of the outlying former textile towns of the ten Greater Manchester local authorities poses huge questions. But the city centre through to MediaCityUK buzzes with possibility. *Original Modern* remains the unwritten mantra *"...and raining"* is my addition. Manchester – the new capital of England as London – the world city – drifts further and further offshore? Why not?

A WALK ON THE WILD SIDE (2008) is an unpublished fragment – part of an intermittent hymn of praise for the City's boho Northern Quarter. I worked in NQ for about five years in the noughties – never, ever a dull moment – the psychogeographer's delight and, for the photographer, rich pickings.

MANCHESTER: CAPITAL OF THE NORTH'S WATERWAYS was produced for *Platform Manchester* – Manchester's elegant new sustainability website launched in 2013. Chairing Manchester and Pennine Waterway

Partnership means taking every opportunity to big up the City's pivotal location in England's canal network.

AND ON THE SIXTH DAY for *Place North West* was a response to the 2008 threats to Affleck's Palace, a famous, cheery indie emporium for goths and teens of free spirit.

I have always found that connecting with the academic world broadens the mind and raises the spirits. Membership of the independent advisory panel of Salford University's *Centre for Sustainable Urban and Regional Futures* (SURF) connected me with very bright people and enabled me to claim that I was on the SURFboard. I was invited in 2012 to contribute to SURF's international MISTRA programme of world cities to by writing a serious piece on Greater Manchester's position on the sustainability journey: this resulted in UPWARD SPIRAL OR LONG DESCENT?

HEAR TODAY for *Place North West* (2007) reported imaginative attempts to capture the city's soundscape.

A WALK ON THE WILD SIDE (2008)

If Jane Jacobs were alive today, she'd love Manchester's Northern Quarter. You can start the day with a fair trade coffee in funky Drip, provoke eco-warriors, pick up a writ from your solicitor, drop in on your architect, check on your comms people, enjoy a drink in a minimalist or kitsch bar, and round off a perfect day – if that's your way – in the gentlemen's sauna – all without leaving the building! The converted cotton warehouse I work in is a thrilling soap opera. Mixed use? I'll say.

Venturing out, you'd be thrilled by the names! *Back China Lane! Tiffany Bling!* The townscape: Brooding warehouses! Edgy graffiti! The people: white van ragtrade men! Goths outside Afflecks alternative emporium!...the soundscape: Madchester ghosts!

In clone town Britain, where everywhere is the same, places that are messy, independent, alive and provocative are precious. Urban design – the kiss of death or key to resistance?

MANCHESTER: CAPITAL OF THE NORTH'S WATERWAYS? (2013)

Greater Manchester has nearly 200km of rivers and canals running through all ten districts. Every citizen of Greater Manchester lives within twenty minutes of a waterway. Does the coming of the Canal & River Trust open a new chapter in the story of the city with more canals than Venice?

It's about time. It's a story with more than 250 years of drama. Ours was the first region in the world to industrialise on an unprecedented scale. Rivers and waterways were at the heart of this. Canals were the dotcoms of their day – extraordinary innovations in financing, and the design of what we now label "critical infrastructure". There have been many chapters – investment and development – the coming of the railways and competition – closures and decline – nationalisation – campaigning – restoration – and now: charitisation.

In July 2012 British Waterways entered the history books. Our canals became the responsibility of what became – overnight – one of England's biggest charities – The Canal and River Trust. The Trust has a ten year contract with government, so is no prisoner of ministers. It inherits the assets and the liabilities. Manchester is a lynchpin of the network – it's where the chocolate-box Cheshire ring and the gritty South Pennine Ring come together. And the Rochdale Canal cuts right through the city centre, linking Castlefield with Piccadilly Basin – a dramatic way of experiencing the cityscape from boat or towpath, walking or cycling, liberated from congested city road traffic.

27 per cent of our assets in Manchester and Pennine (the waterway management area that includes GM) are in poor or bad condition. This is due to generations of underinvestment. And there are "challenges" on every front – economic, social and environmental. Whether it's fear of

crime discouraging casual towpath walkers, or the 483 listed structures in Manchester and Pennine, there is a long shopping list to be tackled. And huge opportunities, too, to revive our canals as vibrant, enjoyable places – contributing even more to local communities and visitor economies: total net spend in the Rochdale and Huddersfield Narrow canals alone was estimated at almost £85million in 2010.

One dimension of the new regime is the creation of Waterway Partnerships. On May 13th, at The Lowry, Manchester and Pennine Waterway Partnership launched its first attempt at a manifesto, 150 participants responding to the call to get involved. It's all about sustainable development. It's about economic, social and environmental change, we decided. In some locations it's about conservation; in others it's time for transformation. Everywhere – it's about innovation – a new chapter begins.

AND ON THE SIXTH DAY (2008)

And on the sixth day?
"AND ON THE SIXTH DAY GOD CREATED MANchester" the mosaic on the side of Affleck's Palace reminds us.

What do Vampire Bunnies, Harpoon Louies, Skinvasion Body Piercing and Vintage 2 Fetish have in common?
They are a few of the forty or so traders, indie stalls, alternative boutiques, purveyors of street fashion, records, and all kinds of exotic stuff in Afflecks. Unsuitable for grannies except the more adventurous and those reliving their Madchester youth: Afflecks was established in 1982.

Where?
It's a typical five-storey converted warehouse in Manchester's boho Northern Quarter where Church Street / Dale Street / Oldham Street / Tib Street meet. It's hard to miss its cheery murals and crowds of youths enjoying a smoke outside.

What's so special about the Northern Quarter?
If the great urbanist Jane Jacobs were alive today she'd love the Northern Quarter…lively mixed use…independent businesses…cafes…bars…clubs…music…the ghosts of Madchester flitting down dark back streets… everything that gives Manchester its edge. The Palace is at its heart.

So what's the problem?
The lease expired last June. The long-running saga of the negotiations between Bruntwood and proprietor Elaine Walsh has been playing out in public, in the press and media. The cast of characters includes Tom Bloxham, who started in business selling posters in Affleck's Palace; vociferous city centre councillor Pat Karney, and the stallholders.

Not another case of tweedy civic society whingers standing in the way of progress then?
Not this time. It's not about the building itself. It's no jewel. Nobody has mentioned bulldozers. It could be converted to flats or offices or retail or a mix with very little visual impact on the townscape. It's about what has become an institution. It's about youth culture. It's all there on the blogs and the online petition with 8000 signatures and endless plaintive eeeeeeeeeks! Catherine: *"without Affleck's Manchester will be just another clone city"*. Julie: *"You can't take Afflecks...I wanted to be thin and work in Topshop before I went to Afflecks...one of the few last places which has a soul in the Northern Quarter"*. Philip: *"It's been part of every teenager's life at one point or another"*. Liam wails: *"Noooooooooooo! Please don't close it! OMG!"*

Beauty and the beast? David and Goliath?
No. Bruntwood does not fit the stereotypical dark forces of rootless property development trashing cities and quickly moving on to the next atrocity...MEN business of the year in '07...innovative customer service...feted for their contribution to the arts...Michael Oglesby High Sheriff of Greater Manchester...actively involved in the city and the region...

What's the answer?
Nobody knows yet. Negotiations continue. We'll see soon enough whether Afflecks stays as it is, closes or moves upmarket with different types of trader able to pay higher rents.

Does it matter?
Yes. It does matter. An important Manchester USP is being cool. There are big questions here: can anything be done to help boho areas on the edge of successful city centres with

low rents, independent businesses and edge; cool, chutzpah? Or is clone town Britain unstoppable? A Starbucks on every corner? Everywhere the same? McWorld?

And history tells us…?
…that cities rise and fall. And so do their quarters. Covent Garden was low-rent seedy a generation ago. Wealthy Liverpool gentlemen used to live in L8. Ancoats was a suburb. Piccadilly Basin was an entrepot for cotton. The Northern Quarter has not always been a Mecca for goths, students and Mac-toting creatives.

Resistance?
Prettification and tarting up the public realm with bollards and seats must be resisted. But Bruntwood can't be directed to have left-field tenants. And hang-outs for tomorrow's teen Goths can't be created by the planning system. This is not North Korea. This is Manchester.

UPWARD SPIRAL OR LONG DESCENT? (2012)

The sustainable development of Greater Manchester

1 The Triple Bottom Line

"Cloud 23 isn't just any bar. Its location and ambience are unique. Floor to ceiling windows offer jaw-dropping view across a constantly changing cityscape" (1)

...and a jereboam of Pommery Cuvee Louise Champagne will set you back £750. The bar on the 23rd floor of the Beetham Tower is the perfect conning tower from which to consider Greater Manchester (GM) – chutzpah, bling and unrivalled 360-degree views of the sprawling conurbation and the hills beyond.

Consider the question of the sustainable development of GM from the perspective of Cloud 23: Do GM politicians, officials, business leaders and citizens leap out of bed in the morning with the war-cry "sustainable development now!"? No – growth is the zeitgeist, consumerism the culture, business as usual the norm, and climate Armageddon the inevitable destination.

This defeatist analysis makes no contribution to advancing the agenda. The narrative may be bleak but there are inspiring stories to be told. This personal perspective concludes with a positive proposal.

GM is not an island. The UK is experiencing the alarming consequences of unsustainable development. The skies are dark with pigeons coming home to roost. We are experiencing massive value destruction of economic and natural capital. Globally, the outcomes of Rio+20 have been irrelevant. Jonathon Porritt, as chair of the now defunct Sustainable Development Commission, worked to help

decision makers and opinion formers embed sustainable development as "the operating system of choice". On Rio+20:
"Nick Clegg and Caroline Spelman are flying the UK's increasingly tattered sustainable development flag" (2).

In Whitehall, "Functional Economic Areas" is the narrow construct of cities and city regions underlining a total lack of vision beyond that of economics. However, Sustainable Development Commission legacies include formal recognition of its principles (3) in, for example, the *National Planning Policy Framework 2012* (4). The principles are:
- environmental limits
- strong healthy and just society
- sustainable economy
- using sound science responsibly
- promoting good governance.

Elkington's *"triple bottom line"* (5) remains a helpful riposte to those who whine that the concept of sustainable development is too complex, too boring or simply defeats them.

It is through the lens of the principles, focused on the triple bottom line, that the question of GM progress can be considered.

2 Greater? Manchester: work in progress

"And on the eight day, God created Manchester"
The Stone Roses (6)

Manchester was the epicentre of the Industrial Revolution, and its extraordinary Victorian urban development has been well documented (7). Its place in world history is assured. Civilisations and cities decline and fall. Manchester has been no exception. Its twentieth- century decline and shrinking reflected global and national economic trends.

Its twenty-first century regeneration has been in spite of the dysfunctional, metrocentric state of British governance. Mrs Thatcher abolished Greater Manchester Council, and with it – city region governance. This has disadvantaged the city in comparison with similar European provincial cities with far greater devolved powers and coherent municipal leadership. It has impeded the possibility of joined-up systems approaches to planning and delivery: GM has ten local authorities. In his 2011 provocation to Liverpool – *"Rebalancing Britain – policy or slogan?"*, former Thatcher Minister Heseltine wrote:

"The government should undertake a a major devolution of responsibility to local government to encourage diversity of administration, distribute capital allocations by competition, reward success and concentrate itself on the spread of best practice. In a sentence, the government should re-create local government" (8).

This is work in progress. GM has been at the forefront of English cities in attempting to construct a new model of joined-up governance: The Greater Manchester Combined Authority (9). The destruction of the Northwest regional machinery, while welcomed by many GM politicians, has left gaps. IPPR's Northern Futures Commission has posed fundamental questions about city region governance, Pan-Northern connections and leadership (10).

In sharp contrast to some of the peripheral authorities, Manchester City Council has benefited from exceptionally strong and consistent municipal leadership. Its recent track record of rebuilding the city centre has been widely acclaimed and there is genuine cause for pride. Between 2001 – 2011 its population grew by 19 per cent, ahead of any other local authority outside London (11). Overconfident claims and the strapline: *"Manchester – original modern"* are open to challenge, however, from a sustainability perspective.

Forum for the Future's annual *"Sustainable Cities Index"* (12) tracked progress in Britain's largest 20 cities –

highlighting their environmental performance, quality of life and readiness for the challenges of the future. In 2010, Manchester ranked a mediocre 13th, with the commentary rightly recognising its success in urban regeneration but pointing out serious failures such as air quality and life expectancy. The Association of Greater Manchester Authorities (AGMA) Health Commission notes that GM has some of the worst life expectancy and health outcomes in the country (13).

Manchester's pioneering *"Mini-Stern"* report as early as 2008 confirmed the city's strengths but warned that the costs of inaction on climate change could be the loss of £20bn GVA over the period 2012-20 within its "Failure to adapt" scenario (14).

There remain immense challenges in critical infrastructure. The Manchester University / Bruntwood *"Ecocities"* initiative (15) points out that 80 per cent of electricity substations, water storage and treatment plants, waste management sites and landfills are located in areas prone to surface water flooding. The areas at risk of surface water flooding coincide spatially with areas of deprivation.

At the domestic level, despite attempts at retrofitting initiatives, a shocking 42 per cent of cavity walls in Salford housing, for instance, remain uninsulated (16).

Generalisations about the private sector and sustainability are of no value. There are distinguished examples of enlightened action. At the other end of the spectrum, ENWORKS has noted a decreasing uptake by GM SMEs of the most basic resource efficiency measures – even those with very rapid return on investment (17). SMEs in the current climate tend to be preoccupied by issues of working capital and decreasing management capacity.

Citizens have choices. Carbon Footprint analysis (18) illustrates the stark reality that no less than 11 per cent of GM CO_2 emissions are generated by personal leisure flights.

The resounding vote against congestion charging in 2008 did not suggest that sustainability was high on individual agendas (19).

In the light of the evidence, it is just not credible to claim that Manchester compares well with cities heading along the rocky path towards a more sustainable future. Can this be the result of sustainability illiteracy?

3 Sustainability literacy in Greater Manchester

"Words-action = shit"
elegantly lettered notice in the office of a Manchester "key player" (20)

There are many references to sustainability in GM policies. The GM Strategy (21) asserts that:

"We will be known for our good quality of life, our low carbon economy and our commitment to sustainable development".

The GM Climate Change Strategy (22) has the excellent strapline:

" Transformation, adaptation and competitive advantage".

On the GM policy agenda are:
- Climate change
- The Green / low carbon economy
- Innovation
- Carbon literacy

Off the policy agenda is informed debate about aviation, for instance. Manchester Airport – owned by the local authorities – has been brilliantly successful in arguing its economic contribution. What is less often underlined is that only 18 per cent of its trade is business. Now it aspires to "Airport City" (23) – a massive out-of-town greenfield office development of the kind that is ubiquitous across the world.

Planning is a way of integrating and mediating conflicting needs and aspirations and shaping sustainable development. Professional planning is being downgraded within the GM local authorities. Capacity is decreasing. The process of "economic development" continues to be in the ascendant in terms of positioning and influence. The inevitable consequence is that it is more difficult to shape coherent, connected, systems based approaches. Great play is made of the importance of evidence-based policymaking. Economic "evidence" on its own, however, is often questionable and always inadequate. Sustainability literacy by definition embraces social and environmental as well as economic comprehension and connections.

Manchester's strong academic sector plays a helpful, provocative role. Centres of excellence such as SURF, CURE and Tyndall are assets. The third sector, intermediaries and partnerships have contributed with initiatives such as *"Manchester is my Planet"* (24).

In GM there are worthy and occasionally excellent initiatives in the built environment, greening, energy, behaviour change and engagement. But none of this joins up, adds up, to a powerful, integrated drive towards a sustainable city region.

4 Upward spiral or long descent: the challenges

"I think that the odds are no better than 50% that out present civilisation will survive to the end of the present century"
Martin Rees (25)

The Ecocities project outlined future climate change scenarios for GM 2050. Its compelling strapline is: *"upward spiral or long descent?"* How does a city adapt to four degrees of climate change? This is a huge challenge – and there is far more to resolve than adapting to climate change. The future will be shaped by turbulent forces largely outside the control of the city region, whatever its governance. David King's "Circle of Doom" (26) neatly summarises these.

Through the lens of sustainable development principles:
- **Environmental limits:**
  How do we reduce the carbon footprint of GM against consumer desires and trends and the retrogressive mantra of growth at any price?
- **Strong, healthy and just society:**
  How can the gross inefficiencies and injustices of increasing inequality be resolved?
- **Sustainable economy:**
  How can the GM economy be retuned to make it fit for a very different future: reversing the acceptance of business as usual, the old economy, and delusions about returning to a pre-austerity golden age?
- **Using sound science responsibly:**
  How do we change the fixation with what is claimed as "evidence" in policy making – "economic data" – to connect with sustainability research, intelligence and science?
- **Promoting good governance:**
  How can the GMCA be strengthened in the direction of powerful city region governance and leadership for sustainable development – against the metrocentric domination of London and the South East?

The sustainability agenda for GM needs to be redirected from the dangers of "long decline" towards at least the possibility of "upward spiral".

5   From rhetoric to reality

"When you have to choose between truth and legend, I say choose the legend"
Anthony H Wilson (27)

There are isolated and unconnected examples of excellence and inspiration. Here are three. Significantly, one is led by the academic sector, one by the private sector and and one by the mutual / co-operative sector.

EcoCities
EcoCities (28) is an initiative led by the University of Manchester and funded by Bruntwood, drawing on the expertise of the Manchester Architecture Research Centre (MARC) and the Centre for Urban Regional Ecology (CURE). The project is focused on the response of urban areas to the impacts of climate change, looking particularly at adaptation.

EcoCities provides Greater Manchester with its first blueprint for an integrated climate change adaptation strategy. Based on leading scientific research, extensive stakeholder engagement, and best practice examples of new programmes successfully piloted during a three-year period, *"Four Degrees of Preparation"* was launched at the *Adapting the City Conference* in May 2012.

EcoCities was financed by Manchester-base property company Bruntwood – a leader in the business community in GM, committed to the sustainability agenda and actively engaged with thought leadership in the city region. Significantly, Bruntwood is a privately owned company, with an expanding geographical reach, but remains headquartered in Manchester.

MediaCityUK

MediaCityUK (29) is a major brownfield development on land adjacent to The Manchester Ship Canal adjacent to Salford Quays. It is a mixed-use development anchored around the BBC.

It was the first scheme in the world to become a BREEAM-approved sustainable community, by incorporating state-of-the-art sustainability factors into the design.

Phase One of MediaCityUK was designed to meet the BREEAM criteria using the valuable asset of water from the Manchester Ship Canal to power, heat and cool the buildings across the 36-acre site. Several of the buildings, including The Holiday Inn and The Studios, use a combined heat and power plant energy system known as TriGen, centralising heating and cooling equipment. The benefits include substantial reductions in CO_2 emissions. The water is returned to The Canal cleaner than it was before.

During construction, the Ship Canal was used to transport materials, reducing the amount of emission from heavy motorway journeys by lorry. Residents, occupiers and visitors travelling to MediaCityUK are actively encouraged to use public transport (including the new Metrolink service). 300 cycle bays have been installed at points across the site.

MediaCityUK is an initiative of Northwest developer Peel, again a private company, with wide geographical reach but still headquartered in the region. Stereotypical accusations of short-termism driven by the vagaries of investors, financiers and the City of London cannot be made against Bruntwood or Peel, both with track records of playing the long game.

NOMA

NOMA (30) is under construction, a new, 4 million sq ft, mixed-use, master-planned redevelopment in the heart of

Manchester: offices, shops, hotels and homes. Backed by the powerful Manchester-headquartered Co-operative Group, NOMA aims to transform 20 acres of Manchester city centre with the distinctive values and principles of the co-operative movement.

NOMA will generate all of its own power, with a renewable energy centre providing for all of its needs through a smart grid. It will be integrated into the existing transport network, with tram, rail, bus and road connections immediately adjacent to the site.

By respecting the heritage buildings, the industrial legacy of Arkwright's historic mill and the history of the site, NOMA aspires to become a reminder of the city's position in global innovation. The commitment that The Co-operative Group has shown to promoting apprenticeships, skills and training through its head office build programme is to be continued through the development of the whole masterplan.

NOMA exemplifies the pioneering stance of The Co-operative Group in mainstreaming sustainability into its many businesses: it is active in campaigning and lobbying for radical change in some unexpected zones, from tar-sands in Canada, to shark eggs in England. Its mutual status enables action in ways that could not be expected of a stockmarket listed company constrained by short-termism and superficial notions of "corporate responsibility".

6   The "Manchester Family"

A tricky question posed by the SURF/MISTRA GM platform is – who is included in addressing the challenges of sustainability in GM? The simplistic answer in terms of public policy is of course the emerging Greater Manchester Combined Authority and the constellation of arrangements that comprise "The Manchester Family" (31)

With the exception of London with its mayoral regime, institutions and powers, Manchester is more advanced in its structures than any other English city region – this is acknowledged by government and all informed commentators. In July 2012, the government's *"City Deal"* devolved further powers and flexibility in resource allocation to Manchester and other provincial cities (32).

Manchester has an outstanding record in co-opting and corralling new government initiatives such as the LEP with a view to ensuring a coherent position in lobbying for resources. However, as a recent *"LEP Family Performance Report"* (33) reveals, sustainable development is not a mainstream concern.

There is no focal point that connects public policy, business, the academic communities and civil society in the pursuit of sustainable development. Diverse and disconnected policies, programmes, initiatives and projects do not add up to a concerted movement.

7 Sustainability Greater Manchester

"Birmingham – that's a suburb of London isn't it"

Terry Christian (34)

Manchester "boosterism" can be a great strength. From its place at the epicentre of the world's first industrial revolution, through decline into a new era of "original modern" – radicalism, innovation and competitiveness have been a hallmark of the city. The idea of sustainable development is no exception:

"We will be known for...and our commitment to sustainable development"

GM Strategy (35).

The concept of a "living laboratory" floated by Manchester University's Dame Nancy Rothwell at the launch of Bruntwood Eco-cities is the germ of a powerful idea. It chimes with the notion endlessly discussed by the tiny, sustainable development sect or "community" in the city that we reinvigorate an independent, sustainable development advocacy body.

Many lessons have been learned from the ill-fated Sustainability Northwest (SNW). SNW successfully boosted the Northwest as the English region that led the way that others were to follow – not only the English regions, but also the UK's devolved administrations. Sustainability Northwest, in its early years, pushed the boundaries of agendas. It enabled the Northwest region to lead the country in exploring climate change a decade before this became a mainstream item. It led debate around "smart development". It ensured that environmental technologies were recognised as a growth area years before this became conventional wisdom. It stimulated and captured thought leadership and engaged decision makers in all sectors and at every level – local, regional and national.

Now we look with envy at the contribution to their cities made by London Sustainability Exchange, Malmo Institute for Sustainable Urban Development in Sweden, Wuppertal Institute for Climate, Environment and Energy and other bodies firmly embedded in their city regions.

Regions are dead for the moment in England and so any attempt to reinvent a regional sustainable development advocacy body would fail. But a GM city region sustainable development partnership could go with the flow of boosterism and the emerging city region structures. Just as Todomorden has invented vegetable tourism, so GM could invent sustainability tourism.

We have immense experience of independent, cross-sectoral partnership models – their failings, their successes and the critical success factors that make them sing. The critical success factors for Sustainability Greater Manchester (SGM) are:

Leadership
Leadership emerges in many different places – in community groups; in politics; at the head of powerful public and private sector organisations. Some leaders are elected. Others are appointed or self-appointed. Successful partnerships need strong leadership.

Vision
The vision must be crystal clear and mission-drift rejected. Visions must be concise – capable of passing the elevator pitch test. The Northwest region has generated more public sector visions than Mother Theresa. Now they are forgotten.

Independence
Gaining the confidence of all sectors – private, public, academic, third and community – necessitates independence from any of them. The agenda is far too important to be captured by any one vested interest at the risk of losing the others.

Timescale
Ecological time, community time and economic and political timescales are never synchronised. Short-term, quick-fix political initiatives come and go and are soon forgotten. Transformational change takes time. Immediate action must be in the context of long-term thinking.

Government backing
England is a metrocentric nation in which government and Whitehall retain power and cannot be sidelined. GM has frequently demonstrated the advantages of government backing for new, strategic "pilots" and initiatives.

Resources
Even in this age of austerity we remain one of the richest countries in the world. Choices about the investment of public sector resources have immense potential to "rebalance the economy" away from the gridlocked, unsustainable dystopia that is London and the South East. The private and academic sectors too have ways of supporting innovation: 1+1+1= 4.

Strategy and delivery
Strategy and delivery must be connected. One without the other is dangerously fragile and undermines credibility. Action is needed at every spatial level – globally at the level of The European Union; nationally, within GM as a geography; and in local neighbourhoods; with local communities.

Ways of working
Aspiring to lead transformational change and to exercise influence far beyond any "mandate" means working by:
- *influencing* opinion and priorities among stakeholders, politicians, government officials, the business community and local people.
- *enabling* projects to be delivered with many partners.
- *enhancing* the work of partners by raising their aspirations towards higher quality outcomes.
- *communicating* and interacting appropriately with different audiences.

Structures
People are more important than organisational structures. Progress is more important than process. Positive change on the ground is more important than strategy. Debates about structures and representation must not be allowed to crush ambition. Despite constipated systems and the dangers of strangulation by structures, process and targets, exceptional people can achieve remarkable things.

Communications
It is not enough to be correct, worthy, dull and sidelined like much of the environmental movement. We live and work in an instantaneous communications ecosystem of many voices and many media. Engaging communications must be at the very heart of the sustainable development mission.

Partnership
Partnership has become an aerosol word – sprayed on everything, often signifying nothing. Aiming for the highest common factor rather than the lowest common denominator is far from easy in partnership working. Mistrust and misunderstandings between the sectors – public; private; third; academic – are serious barriers to progress. By attacking stereotypes, breaking down barriers and creating new alliances, more is achieved with less. There is no credible alternative.

We understand the difference between lowest common denominator and highest common factor. By 2050, a child born today in GM will have reached the age of 38. What kind of future are we failing to design? Time is short. Original? Modern? Who will take the lead in the creation of Sustainability Greater Manchester?

HEAR TODAY (2007)

Why is that man walking down the street with no iPod? ...and without his mobile clamped to his ear? Well, he's enjoying the sounds of the city...the roar of traffic...the cheery chatter of pedestrians...the plaintive cries of Big Issue vendors...the screams of hoodies...the soundtrack of the city...the city's soundscape.

"Soundscape?"
It's easy to be negative about urban sounds. Too noisy, too intrusive, too much. The latest national *Noise Incidence Survey* confirms what we all know: traffic noise is audible in 87 per cent of homes in England and Wales. An alarming 54 per cent of the population is exposed to levels beyond World Health Organisation guidelines for avoiding "serious irritation." Local authorities are expected to produce noise maps. Progress is glacial though. Doing anything about it is lost in the "too difficult" pile. But the flip side of the coin is that soundscapes of calming tones can brighten the day. And familiar sounds say something about a city. The toot-tooting of Metrolink trams says: you're in Manchester. The screech of seagulls says: you're in Liverpool. The braying of ladies who lunch says: Chester. The clack clacking of WAGs' teetering heels says: Wilmslow. Breaking glass and car alarms wailing says...

So nothing can be done?
Wrong! Sounds can improve the environment. And there is much more to this than personal opinion...your idea of urban symphonies is my idea of Armageddon. Our very own Salford University is leading the "Positive Soundscapes" project to build a database of sounds that people say improve their environment. This is not about reducing noise levels – the traditional territory of

engineering acoustics. Their multidisciplinary team brings together an exotic range of disciplines to try to answer the question: How can architects, urban designers and planners translate the research findings into design principles to create sweeter sounding cities?

So designing positive soundscapes could become part of what we must learn to call placemaking?
Or placeshaping? Make up your mind. Yes, most of us have ears as well as eyes...and noses! Buildings and trees can be used to scatter, deaden or reflect sound. Water features and sound-generating sculptures can contribute. Research has already shown that both frequency and volume are important. High-pitched sounds, even if they are quiet, can be more unpleasant than low bass. The whining of a wasp can push you over the edge. The low, steady whump-whump from the heavy metal coming through the wall may be soothing. Surprisingly, the sounds of car tyres on wet asphalt are popular.

Can I be involved?
Yes. Part of the project is researcher Peter Cusack's *"Favourite Sounds of Manchester"*. (FavouriteManchesterSounds.org) aims to discover what Mancunians find positive about their city's changing soundscape and to reveal the Manchester of the ear. He aims to make an audio portrait of the city. A CD, *"Favourite Manchester Sounds"* will be made from the recordings. On the website you can already listen to excitements including buskers, the Metrolink, and skateboarding in Castlefield.

Where will it end? Ministry of Sound?
Not quite yet. We already know and love the planning system. And where would we be without building regs? We plan, design and regulate the visual environment. Built

environment professionals make a good living out of this. But a casual visitor from outer space might reasonably ask: apart from whingeing about traffic noise, why do we completely ignore the acoustic environment in our towns and cities? Why don't we get our mojo working?

9 THE POOL OF LIFE: LIVERPOOL

"Liverpool – a place where things happen usually for the first time", understated the building wrap facing the visitor emerging from Lime Street Station in 2013. That's been my experience – many firsts for me in the place once badged *"City of change and challenge"*. These labels don't begin to do justice to its wild, hallucinatory excess and colour. I'm with Jung and his dream: *"Liverpool is the pool of life"*.

A NEW KIND OF NEUTRON BOMB was a *Building Design* commission to consider the state of Liverpool, in advance of the RIBA's annual conference to be held in the city in 1978.

This was followed by VANISHING TOWNSCAPE, also for *Building Design,* an attempt at a satirical comment on the desperate state of Everton. Reflecting on this piece now, I can't help feeling that it was beyond a joke. My arrival to live and work in Liverpool coincided with the lowest point in the cycle of spectacular decline of this once great world city. It was hard to imagine that it had been the proud home of "Liverpool gentlemen" revelling in their imperial splendour, global reach and superiority to "Manchester men".

SHOT DEAD was a very personal work for *Mersey Minis Volume 3: Longing* conceived as a gift to the people of Liverpool for the city's 800th anniversary in 2007. I was trying to express something about tragi-comedy, bitter-sweet, life-death in what to me always seemed a city of stark contrasts, of extremes.

HARD TIMES – IT TOOK A RIOT opened the book – *Partnership for action – Groundwork: the early years*, co-edited with Phil Barton in 2012. I was setting the scene by describing my experience of Liverpool in the dark days of 1981. It was another country then – harsher, bleaker, sadder and unforgettable.

CITY REGION 2030 – notes for a provocation delivered as a public lecture at the University of Liverpool, one of my roles as a Visiting Professor in 2011 was followed by TOMORROW'S CITY: CAN THE PRIVATE SECTOR DELIVER? – notes for a debate, also at The University, in 2012. The fact that the question could be seriously asked underlines the dramatic transformation of the city from pariah/basketcase status when I first got to know it, towards belief in a successful future – a world city once again? A sustainable city?

A NEW KIND OF NEUTRON BOMB (1978)

The Corporation has spent the last 20 years experimenting with a new kind of neutron bomb. It leaves the people standing but decimates the buildings.

"If Liverpool did not exist", observed a gentlemen named Myrbach in 1898, *"it would have to be invented".* There was an empire then and Liverpool was a port of world importance. It was our link to the Americas and The Mersey was packed with ships from the four corners of the Earth. No doubt some of the delegates to this year's RIBA conference will leave the city with the same thoughts as Myrbach, though for very different reasons.

Ten minutes on the public viewing gallery of the tower at St. John's Shopping Centre is enough to start anyone thinking. Shocked by the dereliction and decay, reeling from the stress, perhaps some of them will be convinced that it is all very well designating it as a Special Development Area (SDA). What's really needed is the recognition that it is a Total Disaster Area (TDA).

Not everybody is convinced that Liverpool, like Glasgow, is a pointer to the end of civilisation as we know it. The Liverpool Publicity Association, for instance, has bitterly argued that:

"For years Merseyside has been labelled with the 'Z Cars County' tag. Allegedly realistic TV drama, misinformed news stories, and reporters out for a cheap jibe are all factors which have contributed to an image of Merseyside being dirty, depressed, slum-ridden and rife with vandalism and crime. A totally false image".

It's not only the media who have had a field day. It's also the social and environmental problems industry. Nowhere, with the possible exception of Notting Hill, can so few people have been researched and experimented with by so many. A decade of *Educational Priority Areas, Community*

Development Projects, Area Management Experiments, and now *Inner City Partnership* schemes has left a trail of reports, yet still the population is voting with its feet. Between 1961 and 1976 the population plummeted from 746,000 to 558,000 and it's still sinking fast, even though new towns such as Runcorn are being wound down.

Not even the Liverpool Publicity Association would deny that the city has its problems. Frighteningly high unemployment, an increasingly ageing population, vast tracts of wasteland, an enormous stock of unimproved hard-to-let housing and shocking rates of burglary, car thefts and vandalism. Liverpool looks depressing and it's no wonder that it has a bad image. At least one national insurance company has special premiums that are higher than anywhere else in the UK for Liverpool postal districts one to eight. Seven out its eight parliamentary constituencies contain areas of "urban deprivation", a neat phrase that doesn't even begin to describe the reality of the lives of the some of the very poor.

It's not all gloom, doom and despondency, however. The city that fathered the majestic Anglican cathedral "to be completed very soon", Gibberd's Catholic cathedral (know locally as Paddy's Wigwam), the Beatles, and an enterprising voluntary section of staggering dimensions, is not quite ready for the neutron bomb treatment yet.

The inner city has been rediscovered with a vengeance and as long as there are still people who are prepared, or have no choice, but to live in it, action will be needed. The really appalling revelation that is beginning to hit a lot of people in Liverpool is that it is not just the inner city that is falling apart. It is also the vast post-war suburban estates such as Speke, Netherley and Kirkby. About 200,000 people live in these. They have already become social and environmental disaster areas. As one community group leader recently said: *"The inner cities programme is the biggest rip-off of all time.*

They've drawn a line round one area and the rest of the place is just being abandoned to total collapse."

To this backdrop of problems, what possible contribution can architects make? Well, nobody in Merseyside would have much doubt about some of the contributions they should not have made. An architectural monument of world class, which no delegate should miss, is the Piggeries in Everton: a group of high-rise flats that has now been evacuated, with the tragic exception of the handful of families who are still marooned in one of them. They will cost more than £1m to demolish or – and it is an interesting thought – they will make spectacular ruins. The Piggeries are the vivid reminder of the real importance of architecture and, of course, housing management.

Then there's the desolation of the vast suburban council estates, monument to the housing numbers game. Kirkby is starring in the smash hit musical *"Love and Kisses from Kirkby"*, currently packing the Everyman Theatre. The show documents the development of the brave new concrete and high-rise world, through the 50s to the present. Not surprisingly, one of the villains is the council architect who was recently gaoled for corruption.

There are the house improvements and conversions which were so badly designed and supervised in the first burst of rehab mania in the early 70s that some of them already need re-rehabbing.

One of the many tragedies of the failures of the 50s and 60s clearance and renewal programmes has been that rehab, in the words of a local group, *"has reached ridiculous extremes. Every pile of rubble in the place is being improved and the dividing line between rehab and new housing is sometimes very shaky indeed."* The city is now building no housing over two storeys high.

No doubt there will be much discussion at conference about that magic phrase "Community Architecture", and one of the many remarkable things about Liverpool is that, in the field of housing at least, it already has a community architecture industry which is very large indeed. Nobody south of Watford seems to have noticed – given all the discussions about new ways of changing architects' relations to a new breed of clients – the less well-off in housing stress areas.

The housing association movement – and that includes a number of co-ops – is of enormous importance to urban renewal in the city. Both the associations that employ in house architects, and those that use consultants, have impressive track records in the quantity and quality of their work. They have been fortunate in being able to marry development and improvement with the nitty-gritty of housing management. Several housing associations are already experimenting with agency design services to owner occupiers and community groups; services that they can back-up with multi disciplinary experience of rehab and conversion. One example is a fine Victorian police station, until recently derelict and decaying, and now well on the way to a new lease of life as a community centre.

If architects really are looking for a new contribution to make in a place like Liverpool, they don't have to look very far – environmental squalor; areas of space left over after planning; derelict and redundant buildings of every conceivable kind. The City Planning Department is pressed to encourage major industrialists to take over large advance factories, and has to worry about uses for hundreds of bits of disused land and thousands of redundant buildings. Who is to set up the equivalent of housing associations to tackle the problems of small industries and shopping? If ever small-scale socially-conscious property development was needed on an enormous scale it is needed in Liverpool. Architects have been showing the way elsewhere, for instance with working communities in places such as the

Clerkenwell Workshops and the Barley Mow conversion in Chiswick.

This year's RIBA conference should be a great opportunity, not only for the profession to confess its sins yet again, but to take some positive steps forward. There couldn't be a better choice of venue than Liverpool for switching the limelight on to some of the problems, and just possibly, one or two new directions as well.

The authors of the famous SNAP (Shelter Neighbourhood Action Project) report – put it in a nutshell way back in 1972: *"If urban society does not alleviate the despair of individuals in our urban junkyards it will surely reap the retribution it deserves."* Most Liverpudlians will agree that they have been proved right. As the mountain of reports on the city gather thicker and thicker layers of dust on the authorities' shelves, there is no doubt that it is time for innovative action. Who gets a piece of it, and how, will be a fascinating topic for the conference delegates to consider.

VANISHING TOWNSCAPE (1978)

A storm of protest is raging over the threat of the destruction of Liverpool's fine Lyceum Club to make way for a £4m shopping development. And the conservationists are giving the city council a run for their money. But the battle to save the Lyceum has distracted attention from an even more serious threat to what's left of the city's architectural heritage.

Haigh, Canterbury and Crosbie Heights, three fourteen-storey maisonette blocks in Everton, completed in 1966, could be up for grabs to the highest bidder. Already, one councillor has warned: *"You don't know who will offer to buy them, if anyone does. It may be a scrap metal dealer who rips out all that he wants and leaves the flats even more derelict than they are now."*

And a well-known conservationist told *Building Design*: *"It's disgraceful the state they've been allowed to reach... particularly as they're a classic example of the design philosophy of their era. The articulation of the facades is exceptionally well handled. And these blocks have a real place in the hearts and minds of every Liverpudlian. Their destruction would leave a glaring gap in the skyline of Everton. The townscape is, and should remain, predominantly high-rise."*

Sensitive restoration of the derelict and vandalised blocks would be expensive. But demolition could cost up to £1m and there are still 48 years of loan charges for the city to pay off.

Architectural critic Dr C****** J***** has a novel suggestion: *"As ruins, they'd be the quintesssential symbol of Merseyside in the 80s. These blocks are the ultimate in far-out pre-post-modern-last-past-the-post. The garbage chutes are the most exciting semiological juxtaposition outside of a Los Angeles ghetto. The 14th-floor graffiti integrates acrobatics and street art by people re-installing the street they never had – pure neo-Dada. And the* *smashed-in lifts are new dimensions in populist de-architecture. Far out".*

Unfortunately, none of the handful of tenants still living in the blocks could bring themselves to comment on the possibility of their conservation – at least, not in terms printable in a respectable newspaper like this.

But there is one ray of hope for The Heights. A local activist may have found the answer. *"What's needed"*, he said, *"is a new use for these new buildings. I'm into city farming. If my calculations are right, it might be possible to breed animals small enough to fit into the lifts – the blocks would make fantastic piggeries".*

SHOT DEAD (2007)

Head resting on the cold white tiles above the urinal as he pissed. Fag smouldering. Eyes shut. Tears rolling down his pale cheeks. Strangely quiet through in the bar, for a Tuesday night, after work. Talking, murmuring. No laughing and shouting. Violently-crumpled Walkers crisp packets expanding in slow-motion from the big green ashtrays. Droplets of bitter cruising down the pint glasses. Soaked up by the Higsons beer mats featuring cartoon Liverpool characters: Pierre Head, Anne Field. Pall of blue ciggy smoke softening the shiny mahogany bar, the copper table tops, the nicotine ceiling.

The Grapes in Matthew Street. Not just another quick pint on the way home on a winter Tuesday. Not just another Tuesday. Tuesday December 9th 1980. The day John Lennon died. The day John Lennon was shot dead in New York. The Grapes, only a few yards from where it began, the Cavern. Where it began, the long and winding road to fame, celebrity, death – gunned down in the street by a maniac.

People coming in for a drink. Or something. To be with other people. To be in a crowd. To be in Matthew Street. Some of them weeping. Shock, sadness, loss.

Street door bursts noisily open. Heads turn. It's the woman who sells the Echo, a bundle of papers under her arms. "*Echo! Echo! Echo!*" Front page banner headline screams "JOHN LENNON SHOT DEAD CRAZED GUNMAN CHARGED."

"*Hey doll*", shouts a drinker, "*gimmeallofthem...be worth a lot one day*". Muted snorts of laughter. Heads shaking in disbelief. This is Liverpool. Imagine.

HARD TIMES: IT TOOK A RIOT (2012)

"Where there is discord, may we bring harmony. Where there is error, may we bring truth. Where there is doubt, may we bring faith. And where there is despair, may we bring hope" – Margaret Thatcher on the steps of 10 Downing Street on her first day as Prime Minister, 4th May 1979. I watched her, on a black and white television, with despairing friends in Liverpool.

Fast forward to July 5th 1981. I picked my way along Upper Parliament Street avoiding the coils of fire hoses, burned out cars, dozens of police vehicles, fire engines – lights still flashing – and knots of police, firemen and people watching and waiting. I can still remember the acrid smell and the unforgettable sight of The Rialto and other fine buildings – relics of Liverpool's imperial glory days – wrecked and still burning.

Rioting over the weekend and over what was to become a nine-day period resulted in pitched battles between the police and the rioters; death, injury, looting; more than 500 arrests, and the police using CS gas for the first time outside Northern Ireland. Back in the office, we looked across the street as our friendly paper shop proprietor struggled to fix corrugated iron to protect his windows and his livelihood.

None of us knew it at the time: this was a momentous moment in the evolution of what was to become Groundwork. It brought Michael Heseltine to Liverpool for his blitzkrieg as "Minister for Merseyside":

"Alone, every night, as the meetings were over, I would stand with a glass of wine in my hand, looking out at the magnificent views over the river, and ask myself what had gone wrong with this great English city…in truth, everything had gone wrong".

People were voting with their feet – 10,000 a year were abandoning Liverpool. Factories were closing by the day. Buildings and land, including magnificent assets such as The

Albert Dock, lay derelict. Perceptions of the city were tragicomic, expressed perfectly in Bleasdale's TV series *"Boys from the Blackstuff"*, gifting the world the plight of unemployed tarmac layer Yosser Hughes and *"Giz a job"*.

I had many personal experiences of the grotesque absurdity of it all. Just one: The Trotskyist Militants had successfully used entryist tactics to take over the City Council or "Corpy" as it was universally known. Derek Hatton had emerged as the Deputy Leader and their charismatic mouthpiece. I was working with co-operative housing groups. Liverpool led the country in co-operatives controlled by the tenants, in stark contrast to what had degenerated into a failed centralist model of municipal housing. Militant would have none of it and was resolutely set against co-operatives and for a return to Soviet municipal values. I was despatched by my boss at MIH, as it then was, to negotiate with Derek so as to salvage some at least of our emerging co-ops. I arranged to meet him in the housing department in Kirkby, one of the City's desolate and unloved overspill estates. He was then – notionally and ironically – a community development worker. In the degrading waiting room of one of Knowsley's third-world housing offices I tackled the abusive receptionist protected from the tenants by steel grilles. Finally, I met Derek and was subjected – in this monument to municipal folly – to a stream-of consciousness tirade on the revisionist infamies of housing associations, co-operatives and everything else that deviated from the Militant way.

Heseltine in Liverpool was more than a breath of fresh air – a hurricane. One encounter narrowly avoided being severely career-limiting for me. One of my responsibilities was a "job creation scheme" opening up a riverside walk alongside The Mersey at Otterspool. We were very proud of this – tight and experienced site managers; lavish funding from the nascent

Merseyside Development Corporation (including a shiny new yellow JCB straight out of the showroom). Best of all – a respectable proportion of our previously unemployed workforce progressed into "real jobs". The construction of Heseltine's courageous International Garden Festival was beginning just over our site fence – we supplied tried-and-tested labour to the contractors. The great man was to visit us as an exemplar and I had master planned his visit down to the finest detail. Our bolshie and sometimes dope-smoking "trainees" had agreed that they would work like the furies when he appeared – provided they could knock off for the rest of the day at 2.00pm – a satisfactory deal. And we were to be alerted when the black government car approached by one of our boys with a walkie-talkie: down with the teas, fags and joints and on to the site...a clever plan. But he arrived – unannounced – from the wrong direction! Just – and only just – we got our performance together while the great man was distracted by the accompanying press and TV crews.

Heseltine's outstanding contribution to the renaissance of Liverpool and the initiatives that he launched at this time have been well documented and are well known. The Merseyside Taskforce – senior civil servants were winkled out of their Whitehall bunkers and confronted with stark realities, provocative people and his insistence on action; The International Garden Festival – at the time a triumph over cynicism and outright contempt for trees became a huge, popular success; The Mersey Basin Campaign tackled the shame of a river system that he famously described as *"a disgrace to a civilised society"*.

These were innovative initiatives embracing radical concepts: the concept of partnership working across the sectors – public, private and voluntary, on the grounds that the job was far too big to be left to any one of these and all had a contribution to make; the concept that environmental improvement was a precursor of economic development – the two inextricably linked. These were fundamental underpinnings of what was to become the Groundwork approach. The first Groundwork strapline was *"Partnership for Action"*. The first logo was trees mirrored by a factory silhouette.

I was vaguely aware of the coming of Groundwork St Helens and Knowsley in 1981, but these connections did not really fuse for me until 1984. By then I was in Macclesfield as Executive Director of Groundwork Macclesfield – one of the second wave of Groundwork Trusts – the Northwest five – initiated by Heseltine who had been inspired by John Handley's progress at Operation Groundwork. June 18th: I watched in amazement as an endless convoy of Merseyside police vehicles snaked up Kerridge Hill – the back way – avoiding the media. They were heading to what was to become The Battle of Orgreave – transporting the Merseyside contingent to join the thousands of other police officers from all over England who were to battle with more than 5000 pickets. In Liverpool it had been youths versus the police. In Yorkshire, it was the miners. CS gas was the innovation in Liverpool; short shield squads (police in riot gear with batons and short shields) were the new dimension in Yorkshire.

Dark days. But no, even the most right-on of my colleagues did not feel that we lived in a police state. But we did believe that environmental degradation was a festering challenge and that positive change was possible. As I became part of the growing little family that was Groundwork Northwest I began to understand something of the diversity of The Northwest – St. Helens and Knowsley, Wigan and Macclesfield, Salford, Trafford, Oldham, Rochdale and Rossendale felt like separate places with their own people. But we shared the history of our region, the first in the world to industrialise on a massive scale. And we understood that one of its legacies was environmental degradation. And that the second Industrial Revolution seemed a long time coming – with the human fallout of unemployment, poverty and low aspirations.

At the heart of what had been described as early as 1984 as *"This great movement of ours"* (tongue in cheek but prescient) was John Davidson, or more accurately, John with his wife Joan. Despite his self-deprecating line – classic quote *"I didn't get where I am today by knowing what I'm talking about"*, he was the charismatic leader of Groundwork Northwest. He was masterly in enthusing and encouraging just about anybody who came his way. Through him, Joan helped us to appreciate something of the bigger picture; her international work, research, writing and journalism made vivid connections between the local (our work in Groundwork) and the global (the emerging issues of people, planet and prosperity).

These were the best of times (as well as being the worst of times) for those of us who were developing our careers in changing the world. We now know that a butterfly flapping its wings in an Amazonian rainforest is connected to the balanced diet of a pie in each hand in Wigan. Everything is connected. Everything is cyclical. In 2011 I found myself at a session with Heseltine in Liverpool – back again, and still rattling the cages. Deja Vu.

CITY REGION 2030 (2011)

Ambitions for the Liverpool city region for 2030

Slide 1: Spider

The answer in ten minutes…as a chief executive I used to work for said memorably to me: *"I certainly didn't get where I am today by knowing what I'm talking about"* …I've always found that an inspiring thought, so in that spirit…here's a provocation.

Let's begin with Liverpool the brand:
- Second City (of the British Empire)
- Third city (of the Empire)
- Seaport
- Pool of life
- Basket case
- *"At least it's not Basildon"* (dictionary of urbanism)
- Thinner city
- City of change and challenge
- Edge city
- Livercool
- Centre of the creative universe
- European Capital of Culture
- The world in one city

…the list does not include some of the descriptors not appropriate in genteel company like this.
   Liverpool can be viewed through many different lenses:
- Victim: cracked NHS-issue spectacles – *"Liverpool is different"* mantra
- Romantic slush / pub singing glasses: rose-tinted
- Livercool: mirrored shades, rock 'n' roll, swagger
- Cheeky scouser: Ken Dodd novelty glasses… with integrated red nose and moustache
   …and today's zeitgeist is of course…

- The digital single lens reflex camera lens: in the hands of a European cultural tourist roaming the waterfront.
- But we're here to explore the city region 2030…a new type of lens, maybe? We'll come to that in a minute.
- What's so special about Liverpool?
- Less organised crime than Naples
- Better football than Marseilles
- More democratic than Dubai
- At 801, older than Rotterdam
- More listed buildings than Glasgow
- *Superlambananas* more popular than Manchester *B of the Bang*
- And, of course, the most famous ferry in the world

Slide 2: Liverpool under water
However…
- As the sky grows dark with Nassim Nicolas Taleb's black swans coming home to roost
- Denial and paralysis in the face of climate change prevails
- The SUN screams…*"Scumbag millionaires – shamed bank bosses 'sorry' for crisis"*
- Investment bankers have supplanted hoodies as the new pariahs…are issued with ASBOS and are cleaning dog poo from the streets (well, I made that up, but it's a cheery image)
- Tinning the voids…it's not just houses that are being tinned now, it's high street stores like Woolworths, which began here in Liverpool
- Doesn't look too good for Liverpool in the short run:
- Centre for Cities tells us that Liverpool is in the economic red light zone, the most vulnerable zone alongside Belfast and Hull due to its relatively high unemployment and poorly-qualified population
- And Liverpool is not the only city in England, the UK or

the world to have discovered culture as an engine of regeneration

As this is a university, I will now bring in a proper academic reference...
- Ivan Turok of Glasgow University explains that there are pitfalls in cities pursuing differential advantage:

QUOTE : *"Some common patterns are apparent and many cities seem to be following broadly similar themes"*
How very true – is there any town or city without a cultural quarter? Well Skelmersdale, maybe, but it's only a matter of time

QUOTE: *"Rebranded images need to be anchored to changes in external reality"*
Yes, well, I remember a visit to Glasgow during City of Culture 1990...and my abiding memory is of an archetypal wee Glasgow Jimmie, long raincoat, bunnet, and of course smashed out of his mind drunk being sick into a beautiful new City of Culture litter bin

"External reality"...Liverpool...
- Think tank *Forum for the Future* now annually ranks the UK's 20 largest cities to track their progress towards sustainability
- Selection of social, environmental and economic indicators – environmental impact, quality of life, future proofing
- Liverpool 19th – second from the bottom – a very long way to go to begin to become a sustainable city by Britains's desperately low standards, let alone the leading-edge European or world cities

Slide 3: Mersey – river that changed the world
What's so special about Liverpool? What is this city's number one asset?

The correct answer is the River Mersey

Empires come and go, epochs come and go, we all come and go – we're no more than the ashes of long dead stars after all – the river flows on, River Mersey:
- First wet dock in the world in 1709
- Enabled Liverpool to become a port city, an international city
- And not only Liverpool but also Manchester via the Ship Canal
- Trade, wealth, migration and emigration, languages, music
- The river was trashed in the Industrial Revolution and most of the twentieth century – severely polluted
- And in the last twenty-five years a genuinely world class clean up has brought back the salmon – Mersey Basin Campaign

The River Mersey did change the world – read the book…I make no apologies for a shameless commercial

So what are the scenarios for Liverpool 2030?

All scenarios should have sexy names, so here are a few:

The sinking and rotting scenario:
A future entirely about past glories; sea level rise, extreme weather events as the climate changes; Liverpool gradually rotting and sinking beneath the waves; the indigenous population voting with their feet…not possible? Take a close look at Venice

The shopping is the new shipping scenario:
Shopping as religion; affluent gated communities; the

starkest of social divisions...not possible? Take a close look at Dubai or read JG Ballard's *"Kingdom come"*

The Mad Max beyond the thunderdome scenario:
Anarchy, chaos, tribalism; intelligent design and religious fundamentalism; climate refugees, the elite long since disappeared to the hills with the weapons...not possible? Take a close look at some of the world's desperate failing states

The post-apocalypse scenario:
Extreme climate meltdown; collapse of civilisation; post apocalyptic wasteland...the landscape searingly described by Cormack McCarthy in his novel *"The Road"*...not possible? think Dresden or Hiroshima after the bombs

Alternatively, is it possible to imagine a sustainable development scenario for Liverpool? Is it possible that we could change course from our present completely unsustainable and nihilistic "growth" paradigm? Is it possible that the crushing economic crisis, coupled with some momentous climate disasters probably in London – a Thames Barrier breach – could point us towards the idea of a sustainable city?

So, through a very different lens, the crystal-clear sustainable development lens this time, let's fast forward to some snapshots of a sustainable city in 2030:

Click: The library of the University of Liverpool Department of Civic Design
- In the planning history section we find the *"English Partnerships Book of Roundabouts"* in dusty boxes of material on "economic development". These end abruptly in 2009. Then the boxes are labelled "sustainable development"

Click: the Council Chamber of the Town Hall
- They're having a serious discussion about the next step in city region governance – an elderly councillor is reminiscing about the colonial administration of Liverpool back in the noughties, in the old days... before the Treasury moved from Whitehall to Bootle

Click: the Mersey Estuary
- Peel's estuary tidal installation – the waterwheels elegantly turning – generating 20 per cent of the city's electricity

Click: the Liverpool Institute for Sustainability Skills:
- Young eco-plumbers and renewable energy whizzes being presented with their degrees by an ancient Jonathon Porritt

Click: The Port of Liverpool
- The port and the ship canal buzzing with activity – look at the crowds of visitors disembarking from that solar-powered cruise liner (binge flying and binge driving are a distant memory)

Click: Wirral Waters
- Look at these green roofs and green walls and funky organic structures – and cool, happy people; café society on the waterfront

Click: Granby Street
- Homes and shops and and little businesses in a glorious green setting – and look they've taken the sustainable regeneration initiative sign down – Liverpool 8 finally regenerated after nearly 100 years of trying!

Click: The Ince Resource Recovery Park
- There's a canal boat tied up alongside the train, closing the loop

Click: The Ferry
- People swarming off the trams towards the fast ferries heading towards the ship canal busy with commuters

Click: Lime Street Station
- The signboard flashes with rail links into the European high-speed network – Paris, Rome, Madrid

….and maybe this is really going beyond the pale, but…

Slide 4: Ocean Gateway

Liverpool and Manchester will be connected:
- One economy
- One place – the Maglev hurtling along what was once the East Lancs Road

Ocean Gateway or Mersey Parklands or whatever we decide to call it:
- Green sward – River Mersey, Ship Canal, Bridgewater Canal
- You can roam from Irwell City Park in City Centre Manchester, through the Mersey Valley, through the fabulous Liverpool Waterfront, and wind up on the beach at Formby as the red squirrels bounce happily around
- And this new wonderland will be the setting for a very much smarter low-carbon economy and lifestyle… Liverpool and Manchester together as leaders in the low-carbon renaissance – the new age of enlightenment – a new age of sustainability

Manchester will once again be original and modern, Liverpool really will be Livercool.

TOMORROW'S CITY: CAN THE PRIVATE SECTOR DELIVER? (2012)

The economy is the wholly-owned subsidiary of the environment. This was true when Liverpool was the epicentre of the the first region in the world to industrialise on a revolutionary and unprecedented scale – when the River Mersey enabled Liverpool to become the second city of The British Empire. It is true now in 2012 when the Liverpool economy is again in rapid transition.

A prosperous future for Liverpool can be achieved only through sustainable development. This demands the rejection of business as usual. And the radical prospect of Liverpool, Manchester and Warrington working with – rather than against – each other. 1+1 = 3.

My experience in Liverpool since the very darkest days in the 80s of chaos, riots and the arrival of Heseltine first time round has shaped my thinking. My conviction is that the only credible way of organising our economy, society and environment is by applying the principles of sustainable development.

Our planet faces unprecedented and critical twenty-first-century challenges. Sir David King's *"Perfect storm" / cycle of doom"* concisely defines these as: food production; conflict and terrorism; water resources; energy security and supply; health and education; biodiversity; minerals; and climate change. Global population growth is the driver.

From a Liverpool perspective, there are further complexities. Growing inequalities destabilise our society and increase its inefficiency, as Wilkinson and Pickett have shown so vividly in *"The Spirit Level"*. We have experienced value destruction and economic devastation on an epic scale – thanks to feral bankers, city boys, failed regulation and rogue economics.

The response continues to be institutional paralysis.

Whitehall is hopelessly compartmentalised – Heseltine has described the departmental silos as *"functional monopolies"*. Local government has been reduced to *"clients of the metropolis"* as Professor Karel Williams has said. The government machine churns out what Professor Alan Harding has described as *"place blind policies"*. Then there is the abject failure of the Westminster glitterati to see beyond London as the centre of the universe, the North as failing colonies, shopping as the new shipping, business as usual, and a total lack of vision right across the political divide.

The Sustainable Development Commission has sketched out twelve steps towards a sustainable economy. Others such as the New Economics Foundation are actively exploring viable alternatives to rogue capitalism. This is difficult territory. Beyond any doubt, however, is the overwhelming evidence from across the world that relentless economic growth is inversely related to satisfaction or happiness. Economic growth is not synonymous with prosperity. Or, expressed differently – The Northwest of England does not need to emulate South East England to become "prosperous". Basingstoke is not the apotheosis of Western civilisation. It's grim down south. Our development trajectory must be smart, sustainable.

And the role of business in the leadership of the city towards a very different, sustainable future? In the 19th century, in the city's glory days, Liverpool businesses were global in reach and ambition. And Liverpool businessmen had big ambitions for their city. Look no further than this university and the contribution of men like Leverhulme who founded the first town planning school in the world here – Civic Design.

Now we are told that the city has become over-dependent on the public sector, many businesses are sub-offices of London or the US or further afield, and strategic decisions are made elsewhere. There are not enough Peels – rooted in this geography; ambitious and risk-taking. Now we are told that entrepreneurs must shape the future – the Apples and Googles that began in suburban garages.

So can the private sector deliver? Not on its own, is the answer. Enlightened government, strong regulation, a vibrant and dynamic third sector: all have a part to play. Remember the stirring words of Daniel Burnham:

"Make no little plans – they have no magic to stir men's blood".

10 RIVER THAT CHANGED THE WORLD: MERSEY

"Welcome to the most famous ferry in the World" blares the loop to the tourists and visitors as they clamber on board. *"Mersey – the River that Changed the World"* was the title of the book that we produced as a contribution to the celebrations of Liverpool's successful year as European Capital of Culture in 2008. At the time, I was Chief Executive of the Mersey Basin Campaign. We felt that no one had done justice to the multi-faceted significance of the River Mersey – not the longest or the widest or deepest of rivers, but with huge impact – economically, culturally, and with its environmental quality dramatically improved. Exceptionally, the overused phrase "world class" was accurate.

Part of my job was to speak up in local, regional, national and international fora for the Mersey, the Northwest, and our claim to be an exemplar of partnership working for sustainable development. WHAT'S THE MERSEY DONE FOR US? for *Bollington Live!* in 2007 was deliberately parochial. I was – and remain – a resident of Bollington and had been one of the founders of the community-controlled magazine which has survived against all the odds and continues to reinforce the town's distinctiveness.

The Mersey Basin Campaign reached the end of its planned twenty-five-year life in 2010. MESSAGE TO THE PLANET (from The Campaign) was one of my attempts to distill the lessons of its success in a few minutes – this time at the final Campaign Conference in 2009. 2010: THE END OF A TWENTY-FIVE-YEAR CAMPAIGN was a final note from me on the legacy website (www.merseybasin.org.uk)(2007)

WHAT'S THE MERSEY DONE FOR US? (2007)

Who said: *"The river is an affront to the standards a civilised society should demand of its environment. Untreated sewage, pollution, noxious discharges all contribute to water conditions and environmental standards that are perhaps the single most deplorable feature of this critical part of England."* An eco-warrior? No, it was Michael Heseltine in 1982, speaking about the Mersey.

As many older residents remember, Bollington's rivers often ran a rainbow of colours. Industrial pollution was the norm. One toxic example was kier liquor. This was a by-product of the silk printing at Bollington Printing Company. It poured untreated waste into the Dean. *"Horrible, caustic stuff"*, remembers John Capper who, in the sixties, worked for the Mersey and Weaver River Authority. John now works for the Environment Agency.

The River Dean rises above Rainow before flowing into Lamaload Reservoir. This reservoir supplying drinking water to Macclesfield was completed in 1964, and is managed by United Utilities. The Dean flows through what Bollington historian George Longden has described as *"the most intensively industrialised parts of the East Cheshire hills"*, the industrial valley which was once the site of the second biggest waterwheel in the British Isles. The river then flows through Bollington, finally joining the River Bollin near Styal. The Bollin flows into the Manchester Ship Canal, which leads to the Mersey Estuary.

So, Bollington lies within the Mersey Basin. We are part of the Mersey River system. The town's industrialisation and development was dependent on water power from our rivers. Our pollution and waste flowed through the system into the Mersey Estuary.

Like most of the other rivers in the system, the water quality of the Dean and the Harrop has improved dramatically over the last thirty years. Both are now clean trout streams. Heavily-polluting industry has long gone. In the seventies, a turning point was the diversion of trade effluent from the watercourse into the foul sewer for treatment at Macclesfield Sewage Works. *"This solved major problems with the Dean and Harrop Brook,"* John Capper remembers. Since the privatisation of the water industry in 1989 there has been a massive increase in investment in ageing Victorian water systems. Environmental regulation has been tightened up. Fines to polluters have become heavier, though not nearly as heavy as many environmentalists would wish.

Another issue is diffuse pollution from agriculture. This is washed off fields, into the watercourses. This is not as big a problem in and around Bollington as it is in intensively farmed areas. Ten years ago, the Environment Agency was established as a powerful regulator. Its experienced people on the ground used both carrots and sticks to maintain standards and solve problems, often working alongside the water company United Utilities.

"People in Bollington are very good at letting us know if there is a problem; they are amongst the best," says John Capper, *"perhaps because the houses are very close to the rivers and they can always ring the Environment Agency Freefone 0800 80 70 60 in an emergency."*

Bollington's rivers are now cleaner than at any time since industrialisation. Regular monitoring of their chemical and biological state proves this. There are new environmental challenges though; climate change means more frequent extreme weather conditions – storms, floods and droughts. Substantial investment has been made in our flood defences. Bollington is not immune.

Last summer's drought in the South East was a reminder that water is a precious resource. The less we run the tap in the house or garden, the less has to be taken from rivers and reservoirs, leaving more for the fish and wildlife that depend on it. A running tap can use nine litres of water a minute. It has been calculated that if everyone in the Northwest region turned off the tap while brushing teeth it could save more than 36,500 million litres a year – enough to fill a reservoir the size of Thirlmere in the Lake District! We need to waste less water and use it wisely.

More and more people of all ages feel strongly about the state of their local environment and want to do something about it. The Mersey Basin Campaign supports local volunteering through our local partnership organisations. In Bollington this is with the long-established Bollin Valley Project. The Project's Emma Houghton is a Bollington resident. *"You'd be amazed how many shopping trolleys end up in the rivers,"* she says, *"and clean-ups with volunteers can make a big difference."* Emma and the team also work on habitat creation, tree planting and tackling the problem of invasive species.

In autumn every year, the Mersey Basin Campaign celebrates the contribution of volunteers to riverside environmental improvements through Mersey Basin Week. This year the week begins on September 28th. The Campaign's Bev Mitchell explains: *"We can sometimes help local groups with small grants. We find that with some projects, a little money can go a very long way. Just being able to hire a skip, for instance, can be a big help".*

What did the Mersey ever do for us? The short answer: no Mersey = no river system = no Bollington. Everything is connected. The long answer will be in our book – *"Mersey: the river that changed the world"*. The title says it all.

Mersey: the river that changed the world will be published by Bluecoat Press in November 2007.

MESSAGE TO THE PLANET (2009)

From the Mersey Basin campaign

A lot of water has flowed under the bridges of the Mersey Basin in the twenty-five years of the Campaign. And the world has changed in ways that nobody could have imagined. In 1985, the scale and complexity of cleaning up our trashed rivers and watersides seemed daunting. Over the next twenty-five years we face even more intimidating tasks. We are the first generation in human history to have the power to save ourselves from catastrophe. We must adapt our built environment and infrastructure to cope with climate change. We urgently need to reorganise our economy and society for a low-carbon economy. We know that constant reinvention of the wheel is a waste. So what have we learned from 25 years of our campaign? We believe that the core principles at the heart of our success will be as valid tomorrow as they are today. In snapshots, these are:

Leadership
Leadership emerges in many different places – in community groups as well as at the head of powerful public and private sector organisations. Some leaders are elected. Others are appointed or self-appointed. Successful partnerships need strong leadership.
   Caption: It was government minister Michael Heseltine's leadership following the Toxteth Riots that led directly to the creation of the Mersey Basin Campaign.

Vision
It is easy to be overwhelmed by conflicting ideas, information and distractions. "Mission drift" is a constant threat. So the vision must be clear and unshakeable. Our vision is of waters clean enough to sustain fish flowing

through green or appropriately- developed watersides. The focus of the Mersey Basin Campaign through its entire life has been on improving the waters and watersides of our river system by engaging organisations and individuals in the process.

Caption: Salmon once again in Warrington for the first time since pre-industrial times

People are more important than structures

People are more important than organisational structures. Progress is more important than process. Positive change on the ground is more important than strategy. Despite constipated systems and the dangers of strangulation by process and targets, good people can achieve remarkable things.

Caption: 2008 Unilever Dragonfly Award Winner Amy Preston, an inspiring schoolgirl volunteer

The big idea

The big idea is sustainable development: progress that recognises that the environment, the economy and social conditions are inextricably linked. Sending the bill to future generations is wrong. The Campaign has avoided being sidelined as a single-issue "Green" group by working across the sectors and viewing all of them – including business – as part of the solution rather than part of the problem.

Caption: Northwest Business Environment Award 2009 award winner BDP raises the bar with its new waterside studios

Realistic timescale

Ecological time, community time and political timescales are rarely synchronised. Short-term, quick fix political initiatives come and go and are soon forgotten. They are not the answer to big, long-term problems. The Campaign's design life of 25 years was quite exceptional for a government-backed initiative – and about right.

Caption: The 115-year-old Manchester Ship Canal has a bright future, as there is more incentive to get freight off the roads

Government backing
Successive governments, both Conservative and Labour, have backed the Mersey Basin Campaign. The government appoints Campaign chairmen: this gives them status. The government relationship reassures business partners and sponsors that the Campaign is a serious force. The government has provided essential "core funding" around which additional resources have been packaged.

Caption: Environment Minister Hilary Benn, a contributor to the Campaign's Environment 09 Conference

Resources
The scale of investment in water quality improvements in Northwest England has been massive in comparison with investment in other types of infrastructure. Since privatisation in 1989, the capital investment by our water company – United Utilities – has been more than £8 billion. The economic regulator OFWAT determines this. Alongside the Environment Agency's environmental regulation, this has made a massive impact: shockingly polluted waters have been transformed and the salmon are returning.

Caption: Work on a wastewater treatment works

Strategy and delivery: action at every level
We have understood the importance of both strategy and delivery, and the weakness of one without the other. Action has been needed at every level. The Campaign is positioned globally as the inaugural winner of the World Riverprize: our reputation as an international leader has been helpful. And it has been good for our region to have one outstanding environmental success story. Europe has been the originator of important environmental directives and of valuable

funding and partnerships: through our participation in transnational programmes we have learned from our European colleagues and they have learned from us. We have been active, too, in influencing policy and decisions nationally and at the level of the Northwest region. At the community level the Campaign's network of local Action Partnerships have been led by people with local knowledge and commitment. This has guided our Action Partnership Coordinators in delivering real change on the ground.

Caption: the Darwen Litter Trap: an innovative solution to a local problem

Ways of working
The Campaign has no power and very limited resources. We are not a regulator and we are driven not by profit, but by our mission. We have sought to lead massive change and to exercise influence far beyond our authority. So we have worked in very different ways – by influencing opinion and priorities among stakeholders, politicians, government officials, the business community and local people; by enabling projects to be delivered by the Campaign itself and its many partners; by enhancing the work of partners by raising their aspirations towards higher quality outcomes; and by communicating appropriately with different audiences.

Caption: Delegates networking at one of the Campaign's popular waters forums

Professionalism
Aiming for the highest common factor rather than the lowest common denominator demands confidence and professionalism. In projects, events and communications, we aspire to excellence.

Caption: The Campaign's SOURCE magazine has achieved high standards in content and design

Communications
It is no good being correct, worthy, dull and ignored. We live and work in a communications ecosystem of many voices and many media. Communications are at the heart of everything the Campaign has attempted. We have a carefully targeted communications strategy that is regularly refreshed. We have achieved very big impact with minimal resources. From face-to-face forums through to state-of-the-art social media, we have constantly pushed the communications boundaries.

Caption: Sammy the celebrity salmon, worldwide blogger, with the Lord Mayor of Liverpool

Partnership
Partnership has become an aerosol word – sprayed on everything, often means nothing – at least in the world of regeneration in which the Campaign is a player. The silos within government and misconceptions and mistrust between the sectors are serious barriers to progress. The Campaign has been a pioneer of ambitious partnership working across the public, private, voluntary, community and academic sectors. By attacking stereotypes, breaking down barriers and creating new alliances, more has been achieved with less.

Caption: Speke Garston Coastal reserve, the largest area of new open space in Liverpool for 100 years, made possible by the Campaign's partnership with developer Peel Holdings and voluntary group, Liverpool Sailing Club.

The journey, not the destination
In its twenty-five-year life, the Mersey Basin Campaign has made a big difference to the economy, the environment and the quality of life in our river basin. Salmon have returned. Development no longer turns its back to the water. Greening has replaced dereliction. But this is just a stage in a longer

journey. The goalposts have moved. Adapting to climate change and meeting the ecological quality requirements demanded by the European Water Framework Directive are just two of the big issues for our region in 2009. Are our successors up to it? For the sake of future generations, we must hope so.

2010: THE END OF A TWENTY-FIVE YEAR CAMPAIGN
(2010)

On 31st March 2010, the Mersey Basin Campaign formally concluded after 25 action-packed years. The decision to end the Campaign had been taken by its governing Campaign Council 18 months previously, so as to enable an orderly exit. The decision had not been taken lightly and had followed extensive discussion and debate with the key partners, led by the government appointed Campaign Chair, Professor Peter Batey. The spirit in which the decision was made was one of achievement, success and celebration. The Campaign's final conference in September 2009 was a memorable and fitting marker of the Campaign's achievements and a look into the future. The final edition of SOURCE magazine captured lessons and perceptions.

The Council, partners and staff worked hard over the Campaign's last months to secure a worthwhile legacy. This website is part of it. Every effort was made to complete projects and initiatives or hand these on to appropriate partner organisations in the region. Great care was taken to support Campaign staff in finding new jobs appropriate to their skills and experience, and nearly all of them found worthwhile jobs...continuing, in their different ways, to work for the sustainable development of Northwest England.

The final meeting of the Campaign's Council took place at our offices at Fourways House in Manchester's Northern Quarter on March 11th 2010. A party for staff, former staff and friends of MBC followed on March 26th. March 31st was the last day.

The Campaign's Healthy Waterways Trust lived on...its trustees believed that it still had an important role. Its quiet work as a broker of partnerships dealing with difficult issues was viewed as being specially valuable.

Buckminster Fuller memorably wrote: "...*there is one outstandingly important fact regarding spaceship Earth and that is that no instruction book came with it...*" The same could be said about the complex partnership that was the Mersey Basin Campaign. There was no instruction book, and inevitably there were both triumphs and disasters. But it was worth it.

11 LIVERPOOL MEETS MANCHESTER: ATLANTIC GATEWAY

Liverpool and Manchester together were the epicentre of the World's first Industrial Revolution: the port city linked to "Cottonopolis" by The River Mersey and the Manchester Ship Canal. The continuing rivalry, enmity and disregard of each other's very existence would be inexplicable to the casual visitor from another planet. But it is complex and deeply embedded in the DNA of both cities. Personally, I have always regarded this as reactionary bollocks, tied up with feral tribalism, football, sectarianism and stupidity.

To this day, the "policy community" of both cities churn out dire "strategies" that completely ignore the existence of the other, thirty-five miles away: shame on them. So I have found my involvement in Atlantic Gateway – one of the successors of The Mersey Basin Campaign – to be hugely enjoyable. How much stronger, more influential and successful the two cities could be working together as a global presence! Years of divide and rule by the Whitehall miasma must be countered and trounced – we need to make Sir Humphrey very afraid. We need to get real to the fact that comfortable, parochial political and institutional boundaries stand in the way of progress. Atlantic Gateway rightly has fuzzy boundaries – ideas have no boundaries. And place matters.

TOP-DOWN MEETS BOTTOM-UP written in 2013 for a forthcoming ARUP book links the theme of the transformation of the River Mersey to the wider Atlantic Gateway agenda.

I was invited to present Atlantic Gateway as a case study

of TRANSFORMATIONAL CHANGE to the RTPI Annual Convention in London in 2013 – an event memorable for Eric Pickles laying into the ashen-faced planners.

NORTHERN FUTURES IN A REBALANCED BRITAIN: ATLANTIC GATEWAY 2030 was notes for my pitch at the Liverpool University Visiting Professor lecture series in 2012.

TOP DOWN MEETS BOTTOM UP (2013)

"If anywhere in Britain can develop the critical mass and momentum to become an alternative growth pole to London, it is the Atlantic Gateway."

Heseltine / Leahy
("Rebalancing Britain – Policy or Slogan?" 2011 (1)

Now, in 2013, The Atlantic Gateway Partnership is established with its very clear mission to accelerate growth across the North West of England. It encompasses the two cities of Liverpool and Manchester, linked by the River Mersey and the Manchester Ship Canal. The business-led partnership themes its priorities around growth, connectivity, infrastructure and sustainability(2). And water is central to how it will deliver them, enhancing the environment, unleashing economic opportunity, and regenerating communities.

The partnership works at a strategic "top-down" level – lobbying and influencing government to "rebalance the economy". One priority, for instance, has been securing investment in the "Northern Hub" initiative to improve rail capacity across the area. This is complemented by "bottom-up" work – enabling and encouraging action at the local level. One example is Port Salford Greenway, a green link between the Bridgewater Canal and the multi-modal Port Salford(3) – a major investment by The Peel Group. This will create a safe, green route for walking, cycling and recreation with clear economic, community and environmental benefit, through some of the most deprived areas of the city. The Partnership's innovative Community Environment Fund has invested in this local, but valuable, initiative.

Atlantic Gateway – while working top-down in a strategic context – is intensely focused on specific projects and their implementation by partners. Strategies, policies and plans, however inspiring, are quickly forgotten if there is no action. It is the delivery of projects that makes the difference.

Recognition of the importance of top-down meeting bottom-up is a lesson learned from previous experience of partnership working in the Northwest within the landscape of the river basin, the Mersey itself and The Manchester Ship Canal. In 1983, Michael Heseltine, then Environment Secretary, adopted Liverpool as his crusade in the wake of the Toxteth Riots. He regarded the Mersey as vital to its regeneration:

"*Today, the river is an affront to the standards a civilised society should demand of its environment.*" (4)

He was right. The Mersey stank with untreated sewage. Further up the catchment, the Ship Canal was so polluted with chemicals that it occasionally caught fire. Many derelict and contaminated watersides had negative value and were undevelopable.

Amongst his innovative initiatives was the Mersey Basin Campaign (MBC) – a unique, government-backed cross-sectoral partnership. Its 25-year programme was focused on improving water quality, encouraging waterside regeneration, and engaging all sections of society in the process (5).

MBC began its work in 1985. By 1999 it had become recognised worldwide as an exemplar of sustainable development in practice, as the inaugural winner of the World Riverprize – a decade ahead of the Thames.

By 2010 the Campaign had completed its mission and was wound up as planned. Fish had returned to the river. Waterside investment, development and regeneration were the norm. Liverpool's iconic waterfront was transformed. Spectacular change had taken place in many locations across the river basin. For example, Salford Quays on the Manchester Ship Canal had been rescued from dereliction. The Quays had become a fitting setting for MediaCityUK(7).

The process underlined the benefits of cross-sectoral partnership working and marrying strategy with delivery.

There were important milestones along the way, including:
- The privatisation of the water industry in 1989 which led to a significant increase in investment by the water company United Utilities
- The Mersey Estuary Management Plan of 1995 – an innovative framework for co-ordinated action
- The creation of the Environment Agency in 1996, focusing on better regulation and environmental management by industry
- The North West Regional Development Agency and its multi-million pound investment in the Mersey Waterfront Regional Park, with its bold 2007 strategic framework
- The multi-agency *"Adapting the Landscape"* scenarios in 2009, addressing the challenges of environmental improvement at the landscape scale.

Underpinning all of this was the concept of sustainable development. Cleaning up the river basin was never conceived as a narrow environmental initiative – economic and community benefits were the intended outcome. By 2000, the chair of the regional development agency (NWDA) Lord Thomas of Macclesfield asserted:

"The North West was arguably the first region in the world to pollute the environment on a structured, grand, even imperial scale in the desire for economic growth. This new millennium will be an age when we can set our sights on reversing that process based on the principles of sustainable development." (7)

The demise of the regional economic development institutions and the regional planning regime has left a vacuum in some of the English regions. Austerity is a threat to holistic thinking and there is increasing risk of misguided quick fixes. Atlantic Gateway, however, like the Mersey Basin Campaign, is a long-term proposition. Sustainability is central to the thinking. Through the lens of global competitiveness, there is a growing mountain of evidence that successful cities enjoy quality environments, public realm and attractive hinterlands. In the race to attract talent, investors and visitors, this is vital. The City of Liverpool exemplifies this – 20 years ago, the only tourists were disaster tourists. Now the visitor economy is accepted as integral to the city's future. The regenerated waterfront is the single most significant place asset.

Complacency in the face of climate change is inexcusable, and within Atlantic Gateway vigilance will be needed to ensure that there is no backtracking on investment on critical infrastructure such as flood prevention. By global and England standards, the area is extremely fortunate in water resources which, from a global investment perspective, is a competitive advantage. However, the water company, United Utilities, must continue to be permitted by the regulator to make the right level of investment in renewing Victorian infrastructure to secure the system's resilience.

Detailed studies for Mersey Tidal Power (8) have confirmed its technical, though not its economic, feasibility. As energy security becomes increasingly vital to the UK economy, the Mersey remains a real asset for future exploitation as a renewable energy resource.

There is much to be learned from other places with landscape-scale ambition and the capacity to conceptualise and think long-term while building confidence through tactical wins. Emscher Landschafstpark in the Ruhr (9) is inspirational in its scope, longevity and commitment to innovation. Thames Gateway Parklands (10) was the unifying greening dimension to the Thames Gateway.

A commitment in Atlantic Gateway's commencement business plan was Atlantic Gateway Parklands – now straplined: *"the landscape for prosperity"*. Substantial progress has been made in securing support for this ambition. Its prospectus will be launched to local, national and global audiences in 2014.

River basin management is a marginal, technical and less-than-interesting concept to anyone outside the water and infrastructure industries and the green lobby. This is particularly the case in regions in which water supply is not perceived to be an issue and water quality has reached acceptable levels. No-one ever got out of bed humming to the tune of the European Water Framework Directive. For policy makers, opinion formers, influencers and the public at large, there are many other fish to fry. The Mersey Basin Campaign survived all governments over 25 years and achieved its objectives as it embraced sustainable development in the round. It would quickly have stalled had it presented itself as a narrow "Green" or more accurately "Blue" programme. The Atlantic Gateway Partnership is gaining traction and support as it constantly underlines the mantras that: accelerating growth is the aim, sustainable growth is the only option, top-down and bottom-up are sides of the same coin.

TRANSFORMATIONAL CHANGE (2013)

Case Study: Atlantic Gateway

The brief:
- What has been the contribution of planners?
- Can planners do more to contribute to the successful delivery of strategic projects?
- Do planners have all the skills they need to play a central role?

Two cities – one gateway?

Manchester and Liverpool were the epicentre of the world's first Industrial Revolution. The Mersey was the river that changed the world. This was the locus of an unprecedented series of World firsts…
- 1715: commercial wet dock – on the Mersey
- 1757: polytechnic – Warrington Academy
- 1761: canal – Bridgewater
- 1830: intercity passenger railway – Liverpool to Manchester
- 1847: medical officer of health – Dr. Duncan in Liverpool
- 1853: industrial city – Manchester peaked as "Cottonopolis'
- 1899 – garden suburb – Port Sunlight
- 1909 – town planning school – Liverpool University Civic Design

So, it's no exaggeration to claim:
 "*On the eighth day, God created MANchester*" and
 "*Liverpool – a place where things happen usually for the first time*"

Cities and civilisations rise and fall...in the twentieth century, game-changing transformation was a response to crises...
- World War 2: the Battle of the Atlantic
- 1981: the Toxteth riots – the coming of Heseltine first-time round – regeneration
- 1996: the IRA bomb – the rebuilding of Manchester city centre

...and in the postwar period we have been the laboratory for every known experiment in spatial planning and regeneration – GIA, UDC, SRB, URC, HMR, EZ and many more

Transformational change the DNA of Atlantic Gateway

The question:
"Liverpool and Manchester are only 30 miles apart: less than the distance from east to west across Greater London. They are linked by two straight and flat railway lines, two motorways and a heavily urbanised belt with powerful assets like Manchester Airport. History divides them. Can they go on like this? In a global economy, does it make sense?"

Chape / Wray (*TCPA Journal* 2 / 2012)

The two are also linked by geography, The River Mersey and the Manchester Ship Canal

The answer:

"If anywhere in the UK can develop the critical mass and momentum to become an alternative growth pole to London it is the Atlantic Gateway"

Heseltine / Leahy
(*Rebalancing Britain – Policy or Slogan* 10/2011)

Rebalancing Britain - nobody said it would be easy

The context for Atlantic Gateway's future is... "challenging"...
- Gobalisation
- Climate change – towards 4 degrees
- Value destruction by The City – austerity
- The most centralised state in Europe
- Whitehall – warring tribes / dysfunctional
- "Place blind" national policies – the norm
- No national or regional spatial planning
- London – a state within a state
- Increasing inequality – its human consequences and inefficiencies
- Massive imbalance in infrastructure spend skewed to London and the South East
- "Creative destruction" – local government, planning

One example:
IPPR has convincingly shown that *"Northern prosperity is national prosperity – over 80 per cent of major transport infrastructure spending in the current national infrastructure plan is earmarked for London and the South East, compared to just 6 per cent for the the North"*
IPPR Northern Futures Commission (11/ 2012)

Vision, ambition, investment, planning, design and delivery make great places

Three recent examples:

Cleaning up the Mersey
The twenty-five-year Mersey Basin Campaign – concluded in 2010 – transformed water quality throughout the river

basin and enabled massive investment in waterside regeneration – just as Heseltine had envisage in the dark days of the eighties

Liverpool One and Liverpool Waterfront
A Grosvenor retail development in a class of its own – brilliantly linking the city centre to the revived waterfront – RTPI national award winning

MediaCityUK
A courageous chapter in the spectacular regeneration of Salford Quays from total dereliction in 1985 to proudly badging itself as *"Greater Manchester's Waterfront"* – already more than 100 creative and digital companies in place as well as BBC and ITV on the way

Atlantic Gateway: the partnership

The origins of the Atlantic Gateway Partnership were:
- Peel Holdings' ambitious concept of "Ocean Gateway"
- Landscape-scale scenarios – *Adapting the Landscape* – developed to shape what would have been The Northwest's *Regional Strategy 2010*
- Recognition by business leaders, politicians, the environmental sector and others that many opportunities transcend historic city region, LEP or any other boundaries
- Experience from elsewhere – Emscher Landschaftspark in the Ruhr, Thames Gateway Parklands for instance
  AG is a business-led partnership that brings together politicians, business leaders and others from Greater Manchester, Cheshire+Warrington and Liverpool City Region under the strapline: *"accelerating growth"*

The priorities

The priority themes spelled out in our business plan are:
- Growth
- Connectivity
- Infrastructure
- Sustainability

Sci-Tech Daresbury
One of two National Science and Innovation Campuses established in 2006. In 2010, a new joint-venture company was created to spearhead the longer-term development of the site. Partners are the Science and Technology Facilities Council (STFC); Halton Borough Council and Langtree, a property developer and investor.

The Northern Hub
The Northern Hub is a programme of targeted upgrades to the railway in the North of England. Scheduled to complete in 2019, it will allow up to 700 more trains to run each day and provide space for 44 million more passengers a year.

The Port and Canal Network
The Port of Liverpool and The Manchester Ship Canal are in single ownership – Peel Holdings – and this creates unique opportunities for logistics – transforming Atlantic Gateway's fortunes on the world stage.

The Port – rebranded as Liverpool 2 – is now being expanded in a £300 million investment programme to accommodate the world's largest post-panamax container vessels. By transferring to the Manchester Ship Canal Shuttle, cargo can access markets with huge savings in CO_2 emissions by shifting traffic from road to water. The Shuttle will arrive at Port Salford.

Port Salford is a £138 million project with planning

permission to develop the UK's first tri-modal (served by road, rail and short-sea shipping) inland port facility and distribution park on the Barton Strategic Site adjacent to the Ship Canal. Port Salford Greenway will create a sustainable transport route – for cyclists and walkers – linking the local community to this important employment site.

"Mediation of space / making of place"

Atlantic gateway is not a planning authority. Our boundaries are geographic, not administrative. Ideas have no boundaries. Our influence is international – aspiring to position Atlantic gateway on the world stage, strengthening the Liverpool and Manchester global brands. 1+1 = 3

We are an advocate/champion and sometimes provocateur in the interests of the sustainable development of a place with distinctive economic, human and natural capital.

Although our strapline is *"accelerating growth"*, we do not see this in mindless, narrow, dysfunctional terms. We know that need to continue to move from grey to green. We know about the overwhelming evidence from across the world that successful places have quality environments and public realm. From the very first beginnings of Atlantic Gateway we have recognised that creating the *"landscape for prosperity"* must be the glue that holds the whole construct together.

Atlantic Gateway Parklands: the landscape for prosperity

Much of the language of environmental improvement has been confusing/depressing/negative – so we are crystal clear about our entirely positive, aspirational vision for Atlantic Gateway Parklands… "greening" to:
- Underpin sustainable economic growth

- Enable smart adaptation and mitigation in response to climate change
- Support the multiple benefits of enhanced ecological systems and wildlife
- Help to improve perceptions of place by businesses, residents and visitors
- Provide space for leisure, recreation, play, culture, sport and events connect people to employment, education, leisure and each other
- Engage people and deliver health benefits
- Support infrastructure upgrades and requirements relating to power, water and waste to add capacity for the growth of key sectors.

Now we are working with partners including the LNPs across Greater Manchester, Cheshire and Warrington and Liverpool City Region to develop the concept – and we are working on a prospectus to bring it to life.

And the planners?

There are big questions for the planning profession and its role in England, not least the hollowing-out of planning capacity in local authorities – in my view, to a dangerous level. And there are fundamental questions about the purpose of planning here in England in the twenty first century:

Vision
Where is it? We need grand visions on big stages – Atlantic Gateway Parklands exemplifies this

Paralysis by analysis
Planning should be shaping the future. Too many plans are about what happened in the past – evidence from drawn from past trends – usually downwards in the North

Design and creativity
Where is it? Planning should be interdisciplinary, pushing the boundaries – as Bruce Mau recently said of Everton Park
"Use beauty as a competitive advantage to attract wealth and investment"

Despite the shortcomings of planning today, ambitious, smart, savvy young people still want to develop careers in planning – I know this from direct experience in a client role for this year's Liverpool University Civic Design Spatial Planning in Action live project.

From an Atlantic Gateway perspective, despite everything, we are neither defeated nor defeatist. Transformational change is in our DNA. Geologically speaking, the south is sinking and the north is rising; we need to move faster than geological time.

Remember Daniel Burnham:
"Make no little plans: they have no magic to stir men's blood."

www.atlanticgateway.co.uk

ATLANTIC GATEWAY 2030 (2012)

Northern futures in a rebalanced Britain:

What do we know?
- Economy is the wholly owned subsidiary of the environment
- True when AG was the epicentre of the the first region in the world to industrialise on a revolutionary and unprecedented scale – when the River Mersey enabled Liverpool to become the second city of The Empire
- True now in 2012, when AG economy is again in transition
- For example, the development of MediaCityUK on the Manchester Ship Canal at Salford Quays would have been inconceivable had the water remained so polluted and toxic that it regularly caught fire
- We cannot predict the future – except that we can be certain that the economy in 2030 will still be the wholly owned subsidiary of its environment

My thesis
- Prosperous future for AG can be achieved only through sustainable development
- Demands the rejection of 'business as usual'
- Means planning and implementation by special area-based initiative on the scale of AG
- The radical prospect of Liverpool, Manchester, Warrington working with rather than against each other

Scope of this provocation
- Brief diatribe about the state we're in
- Comment about planning here in England
- Expedition into the future – fast forward to Atlantic Gateway 2030
- Answer the question – how do we get there?

- Outline the critical success factors for area based initiatives such as a taskforce for AG

Context
- Northern Futures debate that began here on 10th Nov with TCPA et al, followed up by Prof Ian Wray's lecture last week
- The recent Heseltine/Leahy report on Liverpool – *"Rebalancing Britain – Policy or Slogan"*
- My experience as a practitioner here in Liverpool and AG since the very darkest days in the 80s of chaos, riots, and the arrival of Heseltine first time round
- My conviction that the only credible way of organising our economy society and environment is by applying the principles of sustainable development

The state we're in
- World population and resources – Sir David King's *"perfect storm / cycle of doom"*
- Growing Inequalities – our society is unstable and inefficient as Wilkinson and Pickett have shown so vividly in *"The Spirit Level"*
- Value destruction – feral bankers and city boys – economic devastation on an epic scale
- And the response? Institutional paralysis
  - Whitehall – hopelessly compartmentalised – *"functional monopolies"* – Heseltine
  - Local government reduced to *"clients of the metropolis"* – Prof Karel Williams
  - *"Place blind policies"* - Prof Alan Harding
  - Abject failure of the Westminster glitterati to see beyond London as the centre of the universe, the north as failing colonies, shopping as the new shipping, business as usual, total lack of vision right across the political divide

Spatial planning
- Predicament of planning is symptomatic
- Proactive visionary planning has achieved great things in AG In the nineteenth century – Birkenhead Park for example – as Prof Ian Wray explained here last week
- In the twentieth – Merseyside Development Corporation's waterfront regeneration
- But in the twenty-first? In England? Now?
- No national planning
- No regional planning
- Recent outcomes of local planning system here have been desperately disappointing – nadir – retail "parks" – a criminal abuse of the word park
- Planning profession is being downgraded and sidelined in our local authorities in the present slash-and-burn exercise
- The dead hand of so called "economic development" is in the ascendant
- Massive public sector resource redirection into London – Olympics; Crossrail
- "Growth" is the mantra
- Growth for the sake of growth (as Edward Abbey wrote) *"is the ideology of the cancer cell"*

Atlantic Gateway 2030:
snapshots from a sustainable future
Ecotopia – the sustainable scenario – rather than free market / Armageddon scenario…
- Brisbane Australia – Mersey the only river to be receiving the World Riverprize twice – once to Mersey Basin Campaign in 1999, now in 2030 for its spectacular triumph as the cleanest urban river on the planet
- Manchester Victoria – HS2 arrives at the regional superhub
- Salford – cyclists enjoy Irwell City Park at the start of Atlantic Gateway Park

- Warrington – guided electric cars whirr through a green landscape of living, working and playing as the wildlife chirrups and the food grows
- Ince – at the Ince Marshes Resource Recovery Park, ships are lined up on the canal, trains are being loaded and unloaded, power is being generated from waste and biomass, materials are being reclaimed, and more than 1000 people are working in environmental technologies, innovation and businesses
- Liverpool Waters – The English Government's zero-carbon Treasury Building beside the Green Investment Bank
- The Mersey – The Tidal Barrage quietly generates the energy for 250,000 homes
- Everton Brow – its iconic artwork book ends the western end of the Atlantic Gateway Park
- and finally – Brussels – civic dignitaries collect the European Green Capital award for Liverpool and Manchester together, as one

How do we reach this ecotopia?

Three interrelated ingredients: sustainable development, decoupling prosperity from growth, the Atlantic Gateway Task Force

1 Sustainable Development
- Principles
  - living within environmental limits
  - ensuring a strong healthy and just society
  - achieving a sustainable economy
  - using sound science responsibly
  - promoting good governance
- A systems approach,
  or expressed differently:
- triple bottom line, or
- not cheating on our children

2 Prosperity without growth

"Society is faced with a profound dilemma. To resist growth is to risk economic and social collapse. To pursue it endlessly is to endanger the ecosystems on which we depend for long term survival' – Tim Jackson

SDC has sketched out 12 steps towards a sustainable economy and there is overwhelming evidence from across the world that relentless economic growth does NOT correlate to satisfaction or happiness
or expressed differently:
- The Northwest does not need to emulate South East England
- Anyway, it's grim down south
- Our development must be smart, sustainable

3 The Atlantic Gateway Taskforce
- An area-based special initiative dedicated to the sustainable development of AG over the next twenty five years
- This has tentatively begun with the establishment of the AG Partnership Board
- Experience shows that area-based initiatives can successfully tackle apparently intractable, massive, complex challenges over time
- One example is the Mersey Basin Campaign
- In 1985, the scale and complexity of cleaning up our trashed rivers and watersides seemed daunting
- By 2010, a world-leading transformation had been accomplished
- There are inspiring examples from elsewhere in the world – in the Ruhr, Emscher Park for example
- In England there have been a series of initiatives – general improvement areas, development corporations,

urban regeneration companies, that have delivered transformational change on the ground
- Varied in scale and priorities but all area-based, changing places
- We have learned (from analysis, evaluation and experience) what are the critical success factors for these initiatives…in my view, the top ten are…

Leadership
- Leadership emerges in many different places – in community groups; in politics; at the head of powerful public and private sector organisations
- Some leaders are elected. Others are appointed or self-appointed
- Successful partnerships need strong leadership
  Example: the Eldonians – community action in Vauxhall Liverpool with charismatic leadership from the very beginning by Tony McGann

Vision
- The vision must be crystal clear and mission drift rejected
- Visions must be concise – capable of passing the elevator pitch test
- This region has had more public sector visions than Mother Theresa – all of them now forgotten
- Now the mantle has been handed to the private sector
  Example: Peel's vision for the integration of Manchester Ship Canal and ports

Timescale
Ecological time, community time, economic and political timescales are rarely synchronised.
- Short-term, quick-fix political initiatives come and go and are soon forgotten.

- Transformational change takes time
  Example: Mersey Basin Campaign's design life of 25 years – unprecedented for a government-backed initiative – was about right.

Government backing
- England is a metrocentric nation in which government and Whitehall retain power and cannot be sidelined
- Government backing for new initiatives is essential
  Example: The Albert Dock would have been demolished or collapsed without the government-backed Merseyside Development Corporation

Resources
- Even in the age of austerity we remain one of the richest countries in the world
- Choices about the investment of public sector resources have immense potential to "rebalance the economy" away from the gridlocked hell that is London and the South East
- Despite absurd rhetoric about red tape, intelligent regulation is a powerful driver of positive change
  Example: Privatisation of the water industry enabled massive investment in infrastructure – as a direct result of tight regulation this transformed water quality throughout Northwest England

Strategy and delivery
- Strategy and delivery must be connected
- One without the other is dangerously fragile
- Action is needed at every spatial level + Globally
  - Europe
  - Nationally
  - Within Atlantic Gateway as a geography
  - In local communities/neighbourhoods

Example: The Mersey Basin Campaign's transnational partnerships with colleagues in Europe raised our game and brought new resources into local projects

Ways of working
- AG aspires to lead massive change and to exercise influence far beyond any "mandate"
- This means working by:Influencing opinion and priorities among stakeholders, politicians, government officials, the business community and local people;
  - Enabling projects to be delivered with many partners;
  - Enhancing the work of partners by raising their aspirations towards higher quality outcomes
  - Communicating appropriately with different audiences

Example: this was Prof Peter Batey's thoughtful analysis of the Mersey Basin Campaign modus operandi

Structures
- People are more important than organisational structures.
- Progress is more important than process.
- Positive change on the ground is more important than strategy.
- Despite constipated systems and the dangers of strangulation by structures, process and targets, good people can achieve remarkable things

Example: The successful regeneration of New East Manchester amidst the chaos of top down initiatives

Communications
- It is no good being correct, worthy, dull and ignored like much of the environmental movement
- We live and work in an instantaneous communications ecosystem of many voices and many media

- Communications should be at the heart of everything
  Example: Small NGOs with miniscule resources punching way above their weight – Sustainability Northwest's pioneering work on regional climate change for example

Partnership
- Partnership has become an aerosol word – sprayed on everything, often means nothing. Aiming for the highest common factor rather than the lowest common denominator is not easy in partnerships
- Mistrust and misunderstandings between the sectors – public, private, third, academic – are serious barriers to progress.
- By attacking stereotypes, breaking down barriers and creating new alliances, more is achieved with less
  Example: All of the partnership work on the Adapting the Landscape initiative has brought together many different interests and has ensured that the starting point for the Atlantic Gateway is holistic

And finally...

- By recognising that these are the critical success factors to the design of the Atlantic Gateway special-purpose vehicle or partnership or taskforce we can look to the future with enthusiasm
- Even in austerity England, ministers need positive new initiatives
- But no room for complacency, no time for default lowest common denominator, no guarantee of success – throughout history, civilisations and cities have risen and fallen
- In its twenty-five-year life, Mersey Basin Campaign made a big difference to the economy, the environment and the quality of life in our river basin. Salmon

returned. Development no longer turned its back to the water. Greening replaced dereliction
- But this was just the beginning of a very much longer journey, and the goalposts have moved
- Now we must adapt to climate change
- Now we must decarbonise the economy
- Are we up to it? For the sake of future generations, the answer has to be: YES!

Here we are in The Department of Civic Design – the first planning school in the world founded by Lord Leverhulme, a businessman. It's right to conclude on an upbeat note so: plans matter, planning matters, planners matter…and my advice would be to remember the stirring words of Daniel Burnham:

"Make no little plans – they have no magic to stir men's blood"

REFERENCES

3 ENGLAND'S NORTHWEST: BIRTH AND DEATH

AN IDEA WHOSE TIME HAS COME (2001):

JACOBS, M (1999) *Environmental Modernisation – the New Labour Agenda,* London, Fabian Society.
BLAIR, T 2000) *Richer and Greener –* Speech by the Prime Minister to CBI / Green Alliance Conference, London, Green Alliance.
NORTH WEST CONSTITUTIONAL CONVENTION (2000) *New Way Forward – No Way Back* Final Report, Liverpool, NWCC.
SUSTAINABILITY NORTHWEST (1997) *Greening the Northwest – a Regional Landscape Strategy,* Manchester, SNW.
NORTHWEST CLIMATE GROUP (2000) *Carbon Counting – Northwest England's inventory of greenhouse gas emissions,* Sustainability Northwest for the Northwest Climate Group, Manchester, SNW.
UMIST (1999) *New communities for the ageing region – Debate of the Age Conference Report,* Manchester, Age Concern.
MORI (1997) *Century XXI – Devolution in the English Regions: Vision for the Future,* London, MORI.
NORTHWEST DEVELOPMENT AGENCY (2000) *England's Northwest – a strategy towards 2020*, Warrington, NWDA.
NORTH WEST REGIONAL ASSEMBLY (2000a) *Draft Regional Planning Guidance,* Wigan, NWRA.
NORTH WEST REGIONAL ASSEMBLY (2000b) *Action for Sustainability*, Wigan, NWRA.
NORTH WEST PARTNERSHIP (1996) *Sustainable Regional Economic Strategy,* Manchester, North West Partnership.

ENVIRONMENT AGENCY (2000) *The Environmental Economy for the Northwest – a driver for economic and social progress*, Warrington, Environment Agency.
VON WEISZAKER et al (1997) Factor Four, London, Earthscan.

MARGINS TO MAINSTREAM (2005):

BURCH, PROF. MARTIN (2002) *Time for North West actors to learn their lines*
SUSTAINABILITY NORTHWEST, (2002) *IE special WSSD edition*
HEWITT, CHRIS (ed) (2001) *Sustainable Development and the English Regions*,
CABINET OFFICE (2002) *Your region – your choice – revitalising the English Regions*, London, DTLR. *Regional Quality of Life Counts – Survey of Public Attitudes to Quality of Life and to Environment*, London, DEFRA/ONS.
SUSTAINABLE DEVELOPMENT COMMISSION (2002) *Revision of the RDAs regional economic strategies and the integration of sustainable development*, London, SDC.

4 PARTNERSHIP – THE AEROSOL WORD

PARTNERSHIP: NO ONE SAID IT WOULD BE EASY (2010):

COWAN, ROB (2005), *Dictionary of Urbanism*, Tilsbury, Streetwise Press.
DeWINNE, T. L. (2010), *Allied Biodiesel Industries UK* available at www.biofuels.fsnet.co.uk/biobiz.htm
LGA (Local Government Association), (2007), *Councils help battle for plain English*, London, LGA.
LEADBEATER, CHARLES (1998), *We Think – Mass*

Innovation Not Mass Production, London, Profile Books.
LOVINS, AMORY, et al. (1998), *Factor Four – Doubling Wealth, Halving Resource Use,* London, Earthscan.
MERSEY BASIN CAMPAIGN (2010), *1985-2010 Mersey Basin Campaign* available at: www.merseybasin.org.uk/
TENNYSON, R (1998), *Managing Partnerships*, London, Prince of Wales Business Leaders Forum.
UNGER P (2007), The Flow of Events in I. Wray (ed), *Mersey: the river that changed the world,* Liverpool, Bluecoat Press.

5 WHITEWASHING THE YARD – REGENERATION

A FAIRY TALE OF OUR TIMES (1978):

1. HOOK, M. (1975) *Macclesfield – the self-help GIA* in The Architects Journal, 12th November.
2. A good, concise official account of current British improvement policy is – ENVIRONMENT, DEPARTMENT OF (1976) *As Good As New-Housing and Area Improvement Policy in the UK,* London, DOE/COl. In contrast, a highly critical view is – NATIONAL COMMUNITY DEVELOPMENT PROJECT (1975) *The Poverty of the Improvement Programme,* London, CDP Information and Intelligence Unit.
3. ENVIRONMENT, DEPARTMENT OF (1973) *Public Participation in General Improvement Areas* (Area Improvement Note 8), London, HMSO.
4. Remarkably little research bas been carried out on area environmental practice. Useful sources are:

ROBERTS, J. T. (1976) *General Improvement Areas,* Farnborough, Saxon House;
ENVIRONMENT, Department of (1976) *Environmental Improvements* (Improvement Research Note 1/76). London, DOE Housing Improvement Group;

MENZIES, W. S. (1977) *Beyond Bollards: Environmental Improvement in Older Housing Areas* (Unpublished), Oxford, Joint Centre for Urban Design Oxford Polytechnic

6 BANNED WORDS AND BULLSHIT BINGO

ARCHISPEAK (1974):

1 KOESTLER, ARTHUR (1970): *The Ghost in the Machine*, London, Pan.
2 COOK, PETER (1971) in Architectural Design, August.
3 CHALK, WARREN (1971) in Architectural Design, April.
4 LANE-DAVIES, HUGH (1972) quoted in Architects Journal, 20th September.
5 LE CORBUSIER (1946): *Towards a New Architecture*, London, Architectural Press.

8 ORIGINAL MODERN...AND RAINING: MANCHESTER

UPWARD SPIRAL OR LONG DESCENT? (2012):

1 www.cloud23bar.com
2 www.jonathonporritt.com/blog/sd-rip
3 www.sd-commission.org.uk/pages/the_principles
4 www.gov.uk/government/publications/national-planning-policy-framework—2
5 http://en.wikipedia.org/wiki/Triple_bottom_line
6 www.pocketessentials.com/music/1903047803madchesterscene/ai.php
7 HUNT, TRISTRAM (2004) *Building Jerusalem*, London, Weidenfeld & Nicolson.
8 https://www.gov.uk/government/uploads/system/uploads/attachment_data/file/32080/11-1338-

rebalancing-britain-liverpool-city-region.pdf
9. www.agma.gov.uk
10. http://www.ippr.org/research-projects/44/7405/northern-economic-futures-commission?siteid=ipprnorth
11. http://www.ons.gov.uk/ons/rel/mro/news-release/census-result-shows-increase-in-population-of-the-north-west/censusnorthwestnr0712.html
12. http://www.forumforthefuture.org/project/sustainable-cities-index/overview
13. http://www.greatermanchesterhealth.org.uk/
14. http://www.greenbang.com/mini-stern-for-manchester_5445.html
15. http://www.adaptingmanchester.co.uk/
16. Reported at *GM Climate Change Strategy Workshop*, Salford 2011.
17. Reported by Todd Holden of ENWORKS, *EcoCities Launch* Manchester, May 14 2012.
18. manchesterismyplanet.com/strategy/greater *manchester-total-carbon-footprint
19. http://news.bbc.co.uk/1/hi/england/manchester/7778110.stm http://www.manchesterclimate.com/node/3709
20. Observed by the author, June 2012.
21. http://www.agma.gov.uk/agma/greater_manchester_strategy/index.html
22. http://www.manchesterclimate.com/node/804
23. www.airportcity.co.uk
24. http://manchesterismyplanet.com/
25. http://www.ted.com/talks/martin_rees_asks_is_this_our_final_century.html
26. KING, DAVID – presentation to Mersey Basin Campaign Final Conference, November 2009.
27. *24 Hour Party People* (2002)
28. EcoCities ibid.
29. http://www.mediacityuk.co.uk/our-community/sustainability

30 http://www.noma53.com/
31 www.investinmanchester.com/news/changes-to-the-manchester-family-of-organisations-announced/
32 http://www.guardian.co.uk/society/2012/jul/05/city-deals-eight-cities-greater-control
33 www.manchester.gov.uk/egov.../6_Local_Enterprise_Partnership.pdf
34 Apocryphal?
35 www.agma.gov.uk/gmca/gms_2013/index.html

11 LIVERPOOL MEETS MANCHESTER: ATLANTIC GATEWAY

TOP DOWN MEETS BOTTOM UP (2013):

1 HESELTINE, M and LEAHY, T (2011) *Rebalancing Britain: Policy or slogan,* London, CLG.
2 http://www.atlanticgateway.co.uk/
3
4 www.peel.co.uk/projects/portsalford
5 DEPARTMENT OF THE ENVIRONMENT (DoE) (1983) Letter from Michael Heseltine and Government Consultation Paper.
6 www.merseybasin.org.uk
7 www.mediacityuk.co.uk
8 THOMAS, TERRY quoted in MENZIES, W (2001) *An idea whose time has come: sustainable regional development in Northwest England* in HEWETT, C (ed) *Sustainable Development and the English regions,* London, IPPR.
9 www.merseytidalpower.co.uk
10 www.metropoleruhr.de/en/home/discovering-experiencing/emscher-landscape-park.html
11 http://webarchive.nationalarchives.gov.uk/20120919132719/www.communities.gov.uk/publications/regeneration/parklandsvision

Made in the USA
Charleston, SC
24 March 2014